EXPLORING CHURCHES

Paul & Tessa Clowney

A LION BOOK

EXPLORING CHURCHES

Copyright © 1982 Lion Publishing

Published by
Lion Publishing plc
Icknield Way, Tring, Herts, England
ISBN 0 85648 929 8
Albatross Books Pty Ltd
PO Box 320, Sutherland, NSW 2232,
Australia
ISBN 0 86760 801 3

First edition 1982
This paperback edition 1986

Printed and bound in Hong Kong

Pages 3–11 Milan Cathedral

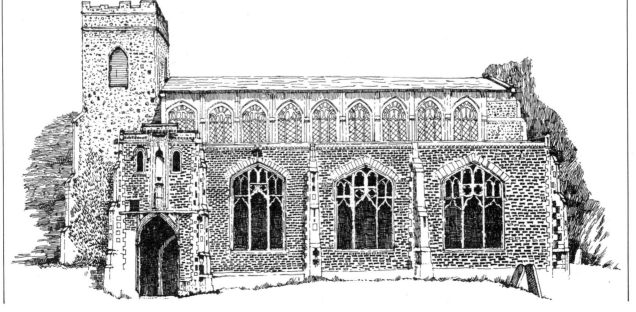

NORTHERN IRELAND

Antrim

BELFAST CATHEDRAL
St Anne
Begun in 1899 from the designs of
Sir Thomas Drew, the church was
continued by Sir Charles
Nicholson, the result being a
hybrid Hiberno-Romanesque style
building which is still unfinished.
At its core is the old parish church
of St Anne, demolished in 1903.

Architecturally, it is basilican in
plan, with shallow transepts and
an apsidal E end with ambulatory
added in the later 1950s. The W
front, with three portals, was
dedicated as a war memorial in
1927. The nave has a floor of
maple and Irish marble, and at its
W end is a maze, a prerequisite of
the medieval cathedral. At the SW
corner is a richly decorated
baptistry, and opposite, the domed
chapel of the Holy Spirit. The
capitals of the nave arcade, by
Morris Harding, represent the
occupations of mankind, above
which are corbels commemorating
leaders of the Church of Ireland.

LISBURN CATHEDRAL
Christ Church
A characteristic example of
'Planters' Gothic', built originally
in 1623 and rebuilt in 1708. The
slim octagonal spire was added in
1804. The first church was given
cathedral status by King Charles II
in 1662, when he raised the Rev.
Jeremy Taylor to be Bishop of
Down & Connor as a reward for
services to the Royalist cause.

The interior has good memorials
and there is a beautiful stained-
glass window presented by Sir
Milne Barbour, a leader of the
linen industry, in memory of his
wife and son. In the churchyard
are the graves of many of the
Huguenots who introduced
improvements in the same linen
industry in 1699, under the
supervision of Samuel Louis
Crommelin, who is buried here.

CARRICKFERGUS
St Nicholas
Originally built 1185, the church
was rebuilt in 1614 without aisles.
Both Norman and 14th C work in
evidence. An unusual feature is
the chancel, which is longer than
the nave and unaligned. Spire
erected 1778. Monuments and a
stained-glass panel in the baptistry
show St Nicholas as Santa Claus on
a sleigh.

GLENARM
St Patrick
Built c1760, this church is erected
on the site of a Franciscan
monastery of 1465, of which only
a section of a wall remains.
Thackeray admired it when he
passed that way, intrigued perhaps
by the portholes in the spire. The S
transept has a chimney, a relic
from the 'laird's loft', as Glenarm
was once a Scottish settlement.

Armagh

ARMAGH CATHEDRAL
St Patrick
Sited within an ancient ring fort,
the first church here was possibly
erected in the 10th C, but of this
nothing remains except perhaps
the crypt, the majority of earlier
buildings being destroyed during
Irish wars. The present cathedral is
predominantly a 19th C
restoration of a 13th C edifice built
by Archbishop O'Scanlon.

Architecturally, it is a plain, but
well-proportioned building
dominated by an 18th C central
tower.

The interior contains some good
18th and 19th C monuments,
including Sir Thomas Molyneux
by Roubiliac. The N transept
contains 17th C memorials to the
Caulfield family, Earls of
Charlemont; sculptured fragments
from earlier cathedrals; and
ancient idols. Hanging in the N
nave arcade is a French standard
captured at Ballinamuck by the
Armagh militia in 1798.

County Down

DOWNPATRICK CATHEDRAL
Holy Trinity
Traditionally it is held that St
Patrick founded the first church in
Ireland here on land granted to
him by a local prince, Dichu,
whom he converted to the
Christian faith. After a period of
Danish attacks, the church was
rebuilt by Bishop Malachy
O'Morgair in 1137. In 1176 John
de Courcy enlarged the church,
and, it is claimed, brought the
bones of St Brigid and St Columba
to lie beside those of St Patrick. The
cathedral was burned by Edward
Bruce in 1315, and again in 1538
by Lord Leonard Grey, an act of
sacrilege to which he largely owed
his execution three years later.

The cathedral received its
present form from the Dublin
architect Charles Lilley and was
built between 1790 and 1827. It
preserves some portions of the
older building, notably part of the
E end, possibly the work of de
Courcy, with its recessed doorway
and trefoil niches. Internally,
arcades survive from the 13th and
15th–16th C, and the font is
believed to be 11th C Celtic work,
rescued in 1931 from a farmyard
after being lost for centuries. The
walls of the church are
embellished with coats of arms of
county families, and several of the
early 19th C box pews have
semicircular fronts. In the wall
beside the vestry door is an
unusually diminutive figure of a
cleric of c1150, and in the porch is
the Cromwell Stone,
commemorating Edward, third
Baron Cromwell, governor of
Lecale.

DROMORE CATHEDRAL
Christ the Redeemer
This is the ancient ecclesiastical
capital of Down, and believed to be
the site of an abbey founded by St
Colman c510. In the reign of
James I, the see was refounded
and the cathedral rebuilt, but this
was destroyed in 1641, and the
present church erected in 1661 by
Bishop Jeremy Taylor. At that
period the see was administered
together with Down & Connor,
but was merged in 1842. Bishop
Thomas Percy enlarged the church
in 1808, rebuilt the tower and
generally restored the fabric; both
he and Jeremy Taylor are buried in
the church. Incorporated in the S
wall of the chancel is St Coleman's
'Pillow Stone' and in the tower
porch are the 17th C font and poor
box.

NEWRY
St Patrick
This was the first Protestant church
built in Ireland (1575) and was
referred to by Jonathan Swift. It
retains in the porch the arms of the
town's founder, Sir Nicholas
Bagenal, marshal of Ireland, who
was also responsible for the
erection of the church.

SAUL
St Patrick
The building is a replica of an early
Christian church and round tower,
built in 1932 by the Church of
Ireland to commemorate the 15th
centenary of St Patrick's landing
nearby, which is the theme of a
window by Catherine O'Brien. The
church is on the reputed site of a
barn where Patrick preached his
first sermon in the country. St
Patrick is said to have died at Saul
in 493.

Fermanagh

ENNISKILLEN CATHEDRAL
St MacCartan
Completed in 1842, the cathedral
incorporates the tower (1637), N
porch and font (1666) of a 17th C
church. Architecturally, a large,
rather plain church in the late
Perpendicular style, its best
features being the inner galleries.
The old colours of the Enniskillen
regiments are laid up in the
cathedral. There are several
interesting memorials, including
statues of General Lowry Cole and
the second Earl of Enniskillen, and
at the W end of the nave the
Pokrich Stone (1628) with a partly
inverted inscription.

ENNISKILLEN
St Michael (Roman Catholic)
Completed in 1875 in the French
Gothic style, it contains of
particular interest a vigorous
sculpture of the resurrection,
unusual for Ireland. The rear of St
Michael's, set on a slope, reveals its
impressive proportions.

Londonderry

LONDONDERRY CATHEDRAL
St Columba
St Columba founded an abbey
here in 546, and the present
church probably stands on that
site, although today's cathedral is
comparatively recent, established
by the Corporation of London. The
nave dates from 1621–33, but the
chancel was built only in 1885–87,
when the original plaster ceiling
was replaced with a wooden one.
Architecturally known as
'Planters' Gothic', a pure Gothic
style of great simplicity. Over the
W end is a tower capped with a
tall, graceful Georgian spire.

Inside there are a number of fine
monuments, and of particular note
is a quaint 17th C memorial to
John Elvin, mayor, who died in
1676 aged 102.

TAMLAGHTARD
St Aidan (Roman Catholic)
Here a monastery is reputed to
have been founded in the 6th C by
St Aidan who later established the
great priory on the island of
Lindisfarne, Northumberland.
Nearby is the SE gable of a ruined
17th C church, and a massive 12th
C mortuary house, shaped like an
ark.

MAGHERAFELT
St Swithin
A Gothic-style church with a tall
spire dedicated to the patron saint
of the Salters' Company who
provided the land and most of the
funds for its building. A tablet and
a window commemorate
Radulphus Whistler (d.1657) of

Salterstown, whose family were prominent in the Magherafelt district until they emigrated to America – where a descendant was James MacNeill Whistler, the painter who introduced Impressionism to the English-speaking world.

Tyrone

CLOGHER CATHEDRAL
St MacCartan
Possibly the first church here was established by St Patrick, or St MacCartan (d.506) who was a disciple of St Patrick. Certainly, the existence of the 9th C 'Clogh-oir' or Golden Stone in the porch of the present church proves that a religious building stood here at an early date.

Today, the small edifice is in the Classical style, built at the expense of Bishop John Stearne in 1744 and remodelled in 1818. It has a Venetian E window commemorating Primate Lord

John George Beresford. A collection of portraits of former bishops, also in the porch, includes one by Sir Thomas Lawrence of Bishop John Porter. The churchyard contains two early crosses of 10th C date.

CASTLECAULFIELD
St Michael
Erected in the 17th C but much restored. It has carved details brought from a medieval church at Donaghmore and a sundial dated 1685. In the S transept of this cruciform church is the tomb of Rev George Walker, the rector who became commander of the defenders of Londonderry in the famous seige of 1688–89.

DUNNAMANAGH
St Patrick (Roman Catholic)
In an area noted for outstanding 'modern' Catholic churches (award-winning St Mary's Melmont, by Patrick Haughty, 1971) St Patrick's is particularly notable for its striking break with architectural tradition in its use of materials: aluminium-faced walls, and brightly coloured, almost garish, stained glass.

Abbreviations

N,S,E,W	North, South, East, West
18th C	Eighteenth Century
c1500	about 1500
Ded Un	Dedication of the Church (e.g. to St Peter) Unknown, lost in antiquity
DoE	Department of the Environment
RCF	Redundant Church Fund

All churches listed are Church of England/Scotland/Ireland/in Wales unless stated otherwise.

Ordnance Survey map references are given for all English, Welsh and Scottish churches. The references are based on the current 1" to the mile series, the first set of figures being the individual map number.

BRITISH CATHEDRALS AND ABBEYS

PLACES TO VISIT

Photographs are reproduced by permission of the following photographers and organizations, and with grateful thanks to the congregations of the churches shown:

The Architectural Association, Peter Minchin, 87 (below), 90
Architectural Press, 91 (above)
Mervyn Benford, 34, 78 (centre)
Stephen Benson Slide Bureau, 91 (centre)
Brecht-Einzig, 89 (below)
Simon Bull, 40 (right), 49 (below)
Camera Press, 60 (left)
Paul Clowney, 49 (above), 62
The Dutch Tourist Board, 45 (below right), 61 (above left), 82 (left), 83 (above)
Mary Evans Picture Library, 50, 53 (left), 55 (left), 68, 84 (above)
Fritz Fankhauser, 78 (below)
Jeffrey Fewkes, 87 (above)
The French Government Tourist Office, 41 (above), 43 (below), 45 (below left), 51, 60 (right)
The German Tourist Office, 42 (left), 58 (both)
Sonia Halliday Photographs, 35, 36, 37 (above), 59, 64 (left), 65, 66–67 (all), 85; Jane Taylor, 71, 76–77
Hamlyn Group Picture Library, 73 (below right)
Michael Holford, 73 (below left), 83 (below), 94–95
Paul Kay, 21 (above right), 89 (above)
Lion Publishing; David Alexander, 30, 42 (right), 50, 53 (right), 70, 75; David Vesey, 21 (below left); John Willcocks, 3 (all), 4–5, 11, 12 (both), 13 (both), 14, 15, 20 (left), 21 (above left, below right), 24 (below left, below centre), 25 (both), 26, 27 (all), 28 (both), 29, 38, 39 (above), 41 (below), 43 (above, both), 46–47 (all), 48, 52 (both), 55 (right), 56, 57 (both), 61 (below right), 63, 64 (right), 74 (above left), 77 (right), 78 (above), 79 (below), 80–81, 80 (left), 91 (below)
Wulf Metz, 84 (below)
David Morgan, 54, 61 (below left)
Press-tige Photos, 11–12
Ronald Sheridan, 24 (below right), 33, 37 (below), 39 (below), 40 (left)
The Swedish Tourist Board, 44 (all), 88 (left)
Derek Walker Associates, 76 (below left), 82 (right)
Western Americana Picture Library, 73 (above), 79 (above), 81 (right)
Liam White, 20 (right)
Derek Widdicombe, 74 (above right)

Line drawings by Simon Bull

Diagrams
Dick Barnard, 16–17, 18 (left), 18–19, 20–21
Paul Jones, 15 (right), 19 (above), 24–25
Roy Lawrance, 22–23, 29
David Reddick, 31, 32, 37, 70
Stanley Willcocks, 15 (left), 19 (right), 33, 51, 57
Daniel Woods, 6, 7, 8, 9

CONTENTS

INTRODUCTION

The word 'church' can mean two different things: a building – or people. First and foremost, in fact, it means a group of people who have been called together by God to form the 'body' of those who share new life through Jesus Christ. A group of Russian Christians meeting in secret in a home is just as much a 'church' as a massive cathedral congregation.

But the word has also come to be used of the buildings in which the church meets. And so the buildings can help us to understand something of the motives of the original builders, the way the building has been used, and the beliefs it expresses.

Churches and cathedrals often form the peak of an age's architectural output. Whether built for the glory of God or of men, they represent a staggering commitment of time, skill and money, and were built by the foremost craftsmen of the day, often employing the most up-to-date building techniques. So simply as buildings, the heritage of churches and cathedrals is awe-inspiring. Exploring churches means enjoying centuries of cultural history. And sometimes the smallest church can be just as fascinating as the biggest cathedral.

But as well as being architecturally fascinating, each church reveals maybe hundreds of years of Christian history. Succeeding generations have used the building in different ways, in keeping with their changing understanding of the Christian faith. And each generation has left its mark on the building. An eleventh-century building, for example, might have been expanded in the Middle Ages, with the clergy's chancel entirely separate from the people's nave; in the Reformation screens, statues and paintings would have been cleared out; in the eighteenth century a new organ might have been fitted and a hundred years later new floors and heating; in the last twenty years all the pews might have been replaced by chairs and the altar moved from the east end to the

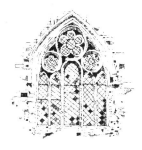

centre of the building. All these changes can be read in the fabric of building.

The second section of this book, The Story of Church Building, examines why different styles of building developed. In most cases the design of a church is a reflection of the way the people of the time understood God and their fellow men, and the way in which services of worship were conducted – whether the clergy said all the words, or the congregation took part, whether there was a procession or not, where the communion table was placed, and so on.

Churches were usually designed with a particular form of service or 'liturgy' in mind. An Eastern Orthodox church separates the priest from the people behind a solid screen. A Quaker meeting-house consists of simple benches facing each other – for there is no 'priest' at all. If the liturgy changed, the building sometimes had to be changed, too. The building itself could also affect the liturgy. Cavernous medieval churches had peculiar acoustics, for example, and to cope with them, it became customary to chant the service.

The first part, the Fieldguide, is intended to be a practical guide to the building and its use. It concentrates mainly on ancient churches as being of most interest to tourists. But many of the same features will be found in different forms of church buildings generally. The section also helps in dating the building and understanding its various parts.

It is worth having a good look at the outside of the building first. The architect will have given a great deal of thought to the overall impression the building gives. If it is an old town church, you may have to 'think away' the surrounding buildings before you can appreciate the church as it first was – with fresh clean stone.

Going inside, first impressions are of great importance. Was the church designed to evoke awe, or mystery? How do the people who meet here week by week feel in the building? Colour, light and acoustics all go to make up this emotional impact of the building. As you explore the inside of the building, it pays to be systematic, 'understanding' first the nave, then the transepts and finally the choir and chancel. Compare the different parts of the building with each other. Are they all of the same period? How does the building compare with the last one you visited?

Then look at the details: the windows, the columns, the doorways, the furnishings. Are there the tell-tale hints of changes in belief or practice, for instance – statues defaced, chapels added, arches filled in?

It is instructive to notice how the church building is used today. Is it a museum or a meeting place? Some seem to be little more than showcases of religious history, full of exhibits, postcards and money-boxes. Others demonstrate a faith that is as alive today as ever.

Exploring churches is a pastime which becomes more and more intriguing. The variety is inexhaustible. This book is a guide to help you see and ask questions. Perhaps it will help you touch, smell, hear and imagine history as you enjoy the design of places of worship. Perhaps too it will help take you beyond the building to a better understanding of the faith that the building was designed to express.

PART 1
FIELDGUIDE

Outside the Building

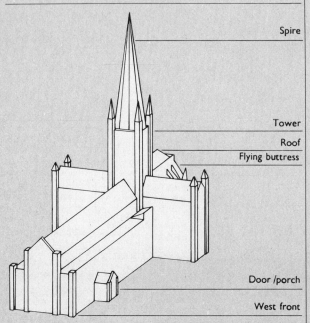

- Spire
- Tower
- Roof
- Flying buttress
- Door /porch
- West front

Towers

Building towers is not easy, as anyone who has tried to build sand castle knows. Towers require carefully-positioned foundations, a good deal of bracing, and well-fitted components. Sometimes they still collapse. In the late Middle Ages when tower building was almost a community competition, towers often fell. Considerable ingenuity has been applied through the centuries to propping up towers and spires. Iron bands, internal truss rods, strainer arches, additional flying buttresses – some towers have them all. And there are some remarkably crooked towers which do still manage to stand.

The obvious functions of a tower are to extend the range from which the church is visible and to support bells. Cathedrals have as many as nine towers, but the two most common arrangements are a single tower at the west end, and two towers on either side of the west front with a third large tower at the crossing. This

The huge tower of the church at Widecombe in the west of England.

central tower represents the church's contact between heaven and earth. Every effort has been made to keep the tower as light as possible; large windows and arches serve to reduce the weight. Towers have often been rebuilt or extended in later periods – not always with a happy marriage of styles.

West Fronts

The most considered exterior feature of larger churches and cathedrals is generally the west front. Medieval builders thought of this façade, incorporating the large entrance doors, as a symbol of the gate to heaven. As such it was more elaborately designed than any part of the building save the altar screen. The structure of the west front sometimes emphasizes the shape of the building behind it; sometimes it disguises it. The twin-tower façade which became the norm in the eleventh century divides the west end into three vertical sections, echoing the internal division of two aisles and a nave. A large window almost always fills the upper central part, sometimes balanced by openings in the flanking towers.

Because it was normal practice to begin building a church at the east end, the west is often dated later than the rest of the church. At times this difference is visible in a marked

The west front of Salisbury cathedral is dominated by the massive spire behind.

change in style. For example, west-end towers were regularly carried higher in later centuries. A Romanesque pediment surmounted by a Gothic tower and Baroque spire is not uncommon.

Norwich Cathedral, though bigger than any parish church, shows the typical cross-shaped plan of European Gothic churches. On the south side are the shaded cloisters: from its beginning, the cathedral had a monastery attached.

Spires

Not all churches have spires. Sometimes this is intentional design. In other cases the spire has been removed, has collapsed or has burnt after being struck by lightning. The spire has often been seen as a symbol of man's aspiration to be united with his creator. It was also a symbol of local pride, and a signpost for travellers. The building of a tall spire made tremendous demands on the finances and skills of a church. The easiest method was to build in timber and then clad with lead or copper; the wind stresses on such a construction are enormous, however, and so this sort of spire had to be drawn tightly down against the tower. If the foundations could take the weight, a spire could be built of stone, but this was expensive, dangerous and difficult. Each stone had to be carefully cut in compound angles, carried up the scaffolding, supported by templates and finally mortared into place.

The small spires or pinnacles at the base of the main central spire of a cathedral were more than decoration. By their extra weight they secured the base of the spire against the outward thrust.

Sites

Churches were often built on an important site – the grave of a martyr, or the site of a previous church. Not all of these locations were really ideal. The churches of Ravenna, Winchester and Ely were all built on marshland. Amsterdam required foundation piles driven as deep as the churches are tall. Subsidence in Ravenna has amounted to more than three feet (one metre) in places. Modern city life poses a serious threat to many old buildings; exhaust fumes erode the stone, vibrations from heavy traffic loosen the joints, excavations in the vicinity can affect foundations.

Many churches are built on hillsides, naturally dominating the area around.

Roofs

Roofs are often covered in lead plate, sometimes as much as a quarter of an inch (almost a centimetre) thick. The considerable weight of such a roof prevents it from being blown away but adds substantially to the stress on the walls. A carefully cross-braced beam structure lies between the roof cladding and the vault of the ceiling, and this forest of wood always adds to the hazard of fire. There are terrifying accounts of cathedral fires in which molten lead poured from the guttering like water.

The massive cathedral of Milan is roofed in great slabs of marble – sloping gently enough for people to walk on with ease.

Gargoyles

On a large roof, rain-water can pose problems. Simply getting rid of all the water from a cloudburst calls for careful design. If water overflows onto the walls or the vault it can cause rot or even collapse. The simplest way of getting rid of the water quickly was to fix great projecting spouts to the guttering so that the water could fall clear of the walls. These spouts commonly assumed the form of fantastic beasts called gargoyles.

Doors/Porches

The entrance doors of the west front of cathedrals were reserved for processions, state occasions and religious festivals. Day-to-day traffic entered in most cases through a doorway on the north-west aisle. This doorway was protected from the weather by a porch. The porch itself acquired a certain significance. Marriages were sometimes conducted there, and it was a common place to seal business agreements – 'by church door'.

There is some noteworthy sculpture in these porches, with two themes being particularly popular. The first is the baptism of Christ, for baptism is the symbol of entry into God's family, the church. The second theme is the changing seasons and their respective labours; this serves to remind the faithful that Christ is involved in all parts of human life.

As well as providing shelter at the door, the porch was used in medieval times for weddings and for trade.

Buttresses

Churches often have thickened sections of wall or even what look like small walls running out from the main building. The one purpose of these 'buttresses' is to give greater rigidity to the whole structure. The greater the weight of a buttress, the more it pushes down and the greater the lateral forces it can withstand.

The massive buttresses of Romanesque churches strengthened the fabric of the building but left little room for large windows. The Gothic builders, by contrast, placed buttresses only at key structural points. The further a buttress is from the wall it supports, the greater its efficiency. The best-constructed buttresses (and interior piers) are solid throughout. But it was simpler and cheaper to make them hollow and to fill the interior with rubble.

The structural strength of tall towers and walls is provided by carefully-placed buttresses.

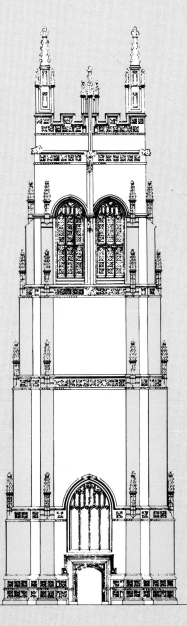

Flying Buttresses

Flying buttresses are strengthening arches which reach from a vertical buttress to a wall, generally to the upper wall of the nave. These counteract the outward thrust of the roof against the comparatively thin upper nave wall.

The aisle, with its low roof, has a thick buttress outside it. On top of this are two levels of flying buttress which support the nave wall and bear outwards on a pinnacled column.

Bells

A full 'peal' of bells can weigh several tonnes, considerably adding to the weight of the tower. In the seventeenth century much ingenuity went into designing mechanical contrivances such as 'carillons' which could chime the bells. These are still used widely on the continent of Europe. In Britain 'change ringing' is more popular; the six or more bells are rung in intricately varying sequences.

Inside the Building

The Crossing

The Transept

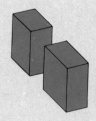

The Nave

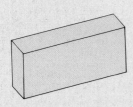

The Aisles

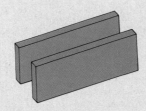

The nave (from 'navis' = ship) is the main area for the congregation. In medieval times it was a popular meeting-place, even for trading. The length of the nave is divided into bays by 'piers' or columns. Shafts which extend up the surface of the wall from the piers or columns are called 'half shafts' because of their semicircular cross section. These vertical divisions are almost always stressed in Gothic architecture to emphasize height. (If they run from vault to floor in an unbroken line they will emphasize the vertical more than if they stop at the top of the arcade; if the piers are composed of 'bundles' of shafts this also contributes to a vertical stress.)

Aisles run parallel with the nave, often separated from it by the main columns. Generally the roof is lower over the aisles; the nave walls above the level of the aisle roofs are pierced with the clerestory windows. Aisles are mainly used for seating, but there may also be memorial tombs, as well as bookstalls and displays showing the work of the church and the missionary outreach it supports.

The intersection of the nave and the transept, the crossing, is a natural centre for a church. It is also the structural kingpin of the building. Here the space opens out in all directions and light from the nave mixes with light from the transept. In some larger churches there is a 'triforium', sometimes a passage-way which runs right round the transept. Get up into this space to look down on the crossing if you can possibly do so. The four corner piers of the crossing are thicker than the piers of the nave arcade. Occasionally arches are partially or completely blocked in to give the crossing greater strength. In some cases 'strainer arches' have been built in. But despite all the bracing and strainer arches, crossing towers and spires have sometimes still fallen through the roof.

The transept crosses the nave at right angles. It gives the church the form of a cross. Some bigger churches have several transepts, sometimes diminishing in length towards the eastern end. The end walls of the transepts can be treated in many ways, but the most common is to have a 'blind arcading' – arches built nearly flush with the wall – sometimes with a large rose window above.

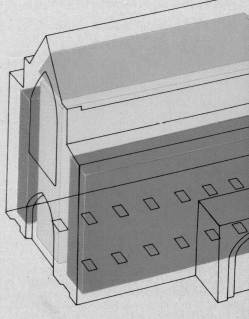

The Chancel/ Choir

The choir or chancel is where services are sung or said. To emphasize the mystery and holiness of the service in Catholic churches, the choir was often separated from the people by a screen. These screens are sometimes beautifully carved – the wood carver's flamboyant challenge to the stone worker. In addition to the screens the choir is also distinguished from the nave by a raised floor; in cases where churches were built over crypts, the level of the choir floor could be six to ten feet (two to three metres) higher than the nave. In the Middle Ages some choirs would be opened at stated times to allow pilgrims to view relics.

The Vault

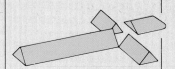

The vault or ceiling is always one of the more spectacular interior elements. From the crudely-hewn tunnel vaults of early Romanesque to the bizarre and gravity-defying pendulum vaults of the seventeenth century, these stone ceilings are always fascinating. The first rib vaults in the twelfth century were a functional solution to the roofing problem. It was not long before ribs were being used for a decorative effect as well as for structural purposes. Short rib sections spread from the tops of half shafts like a net over the nave, each intersection embellished by a carved and painted boss. Vaults were often added later; it was common practice to roof first in timber. Sometimes a later vault does not fit in neatly with the clerestory.

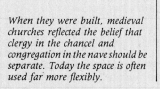

When they were built, medieval churches reflected the belief that clergy in the chancel and congregation in the nave should be separate. Today the space is often used far more flexibly.

Nave Levels

Naves are often built in three 'layers'; at the bottom the large arched arcade; then the middle level of arches, the triforium. Above this is the clerestory – windows over the aisle roof which let light into the nave. Sometimes a fourth division called a **tribune** is added. The proportions of the different levels were the subject of extensive discussion. If the span of the arches in the triforium is too broad compared to their height, the middle section of the wall can seem a bit squashed!

Capitals

The capitals, or tops of the columns, are usually carved with foliage, figures, patterns, or all three. Note the way in which the shape of the capital is harmonized with the figures. Such carving required experience – if the chisel broke a bit off there was no option but to change the design or to start again.

Chapels

Small chapels are often built off the eastern wall of transepts and on side-aisles. Many of these were 'chantry chapels'; they were commissioned in the Middle Ages by the wealthy for the 'chanting' of daily mass on behalf of the souls of members of their family who had died, in the belief that prayers could reduce their time in purgatory. Today they are used for private prayer, for smaller services, or as places for people to come to 'confession', unburdening their sins with a spiritual adviser.

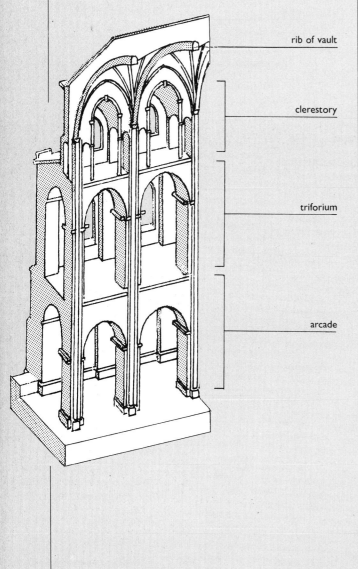

rib of vault

clerestory

triforium

arcade

In this example, the triforium forms a passage right round the building, almost the size of the aisle below it. The round-headed arches show that the nave was built in the Norman period. The pointed windows in the chancel date from the fifteenth century.

The Ambulatory

The passage which runs around and behind the choir is known as the ambulatory, for 'walking round'. In the more prestigious plans twin ambulatories were popular; it was a particularly suitable arrangement for pilgrim churches. The usual treatment of the eastern end of the building in Europe was the chevet or half circle of chapels opening off the bays of a rounded apse. In England there is sometimes a 'Lady Chapel' – usually in the form of a highly decorated extension to the east end of the choir, dedicated to the Virgin Mary.

Moulding

Moulding is sometimes cut from contrasting stone. The horizontal divisions are usually stressed with thin stone mouldings known as stringing. Compare cross-sections of the piers, window mullions (the vertical dividers) with half-shafts, stringing, ribs, and so on. These stones were cut from 'profile templates', so looking at cross-sections shows how the architect achieved his goal.

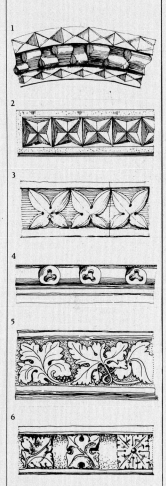

Some styles of moulding have their own names. The 'billet and lozenge' (1) and the 'star' (2) date from the eleventh century, the 'ballflower' (4) and 'vine' (5) from the high Gothic period. (3) also dates from this period, and (6) from the late Gothic.

The Building in Use

The activities of a particular church are represented in the building that has been developed over the years to serve its various purposes.

The local church or chapel is usually built as the meeting place of a local congregation, used for services for worship Sunday by Sunday, for festivals such as Christmas and Easter, for Sunday schools for children and many other purposes. There is plenty of seating for the congregation.

Cathedrals

The Cathedral, usually in a city centre, is the central building of a diocese – the church's 'area headquarters', led by the bishop. Often it is used for more formal and civic occasions. Particularly if there is a choir school, there is stress on services being sung or said on behalf of the community rather than with the involvement of the congregation.

Congregation ①

The congregation sits in pews or seats usually facing one end; or in modern churches and those stressing communal fellowship they may be gathered round a central communion table.

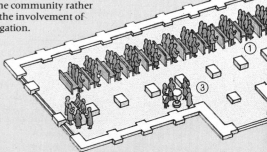

Festivals

Festivals such as Christmas and Easter are celebrated in local churches and cathedrals. **Christmas** celebrates the birth of Jesus; card services, candle-lit services and other traditions make it a joyful festival, often involving the children. **Easter** recalls the death and resurrection of Jesus: Good Friday is an opportunity for repentance and renewed forgiveness; Easter Day the triumphant celebration of the rising again of Jesus to new life as the first of a new creation. **Whitsun** remembers the coming of the Spirit of God to the church. Other festivals such as **Harvest** bring thanksgiving to God; all are opportunities for decorating the church in imaginative and appropriate ways.

Private Chapels ②

Private chapels were often built at the end of the medieval period or in the nineteenth century to say masses on behalf of a wealthy individual, not for congregational use at all. Side-chapels in cathedrals sometimes represent the same belief and practice. Reformed churches discontinued the practice, as it undermined their teaching that salvation is by trust in the work of Jesus, not anything we can do for ourselves.

THIS PAGE, LEFT *In this packed Baptist church at Christmas the gallery gives a good view of the children's nativity play.* ABOVE *The cathedral is used not just for services but also for events such as this international gathering of young people.* OPPOSITE, ABOVE LEFT *Baptism in this church is by 'total immersion'.* BELOW RIGHT *In an Anglican church, the minister leading the service gives bread and wine to the congregation.*

Baptism ③

Baptism is a vivid visual demonstration of becoming a Christian. The person 'dies' to his old sinful life by going down into water, and 'rises again with Jesus' in newness of life. Some churches practice this quite literally with a large 'baptistry' which allows people to go right into the water. In other churches a stone 'font' fulfils the same function more symbolically, and the water is sprinkled. In the case of children, promises are made by parents or god-parents on behalf of the child which are later 'confirmed' if the person comes to full belief.

Choirs ⑤

The choir lead the singing from the chancel or choir-stalls, usually accompanied by an **organ.** Hymns and psalms are a major part of services. In some churches the whole service is sung: in medieval times the voice would carry to a very large congregation if the service was intoned or sung.

Priory, convent or monastery churches are designed for the daily services of a community of Christians who live together. Sometimes they require only the 'chancel' or choir part of the church, as there is no other congregation, so no need for the main nave at all – except for churches at a place of pilgrimage.

Communion ⑥

The **Communion service, Mass, Eucharist, Lord's Supper** (varying names for the same service) is usually a main event in the church's life. It is a 'visual aid' of the death and rising again of Jesus: just as bread and wine are shared, believers share in forgiveness for their sins by the death of Jesus, and in new life by his rising again. It is celebrated from a communion table; sometimes a simple wooden table, or in churches which stress the service as a re-enactment of Jesus' sacrifice a stone or marble altar. In some churches different coloured altar-cloths are used at different times in the church's year.

Sunday Schools ④

A Sunday school often has a corner or room in a church: children are taught in classes appropriate to their age-group.

Main Periods of Church Architecture

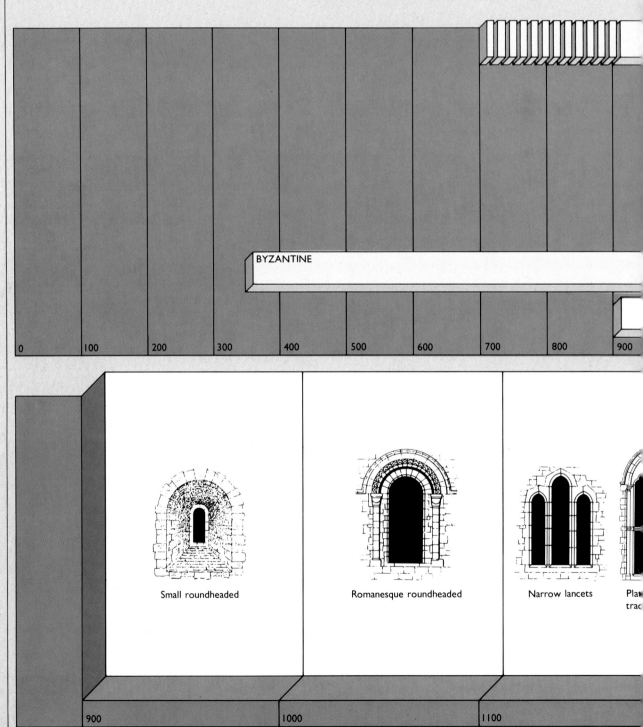

BYZANTINE

| 0 | 100 | 200 | 300 | 400 | 500 | 600 | 700 | 800 | 900 |

Small roundheaded

Romanesque roundheaded

Narrow lancets

Pla
tra

| 900 | 1000 | 1100 |

22

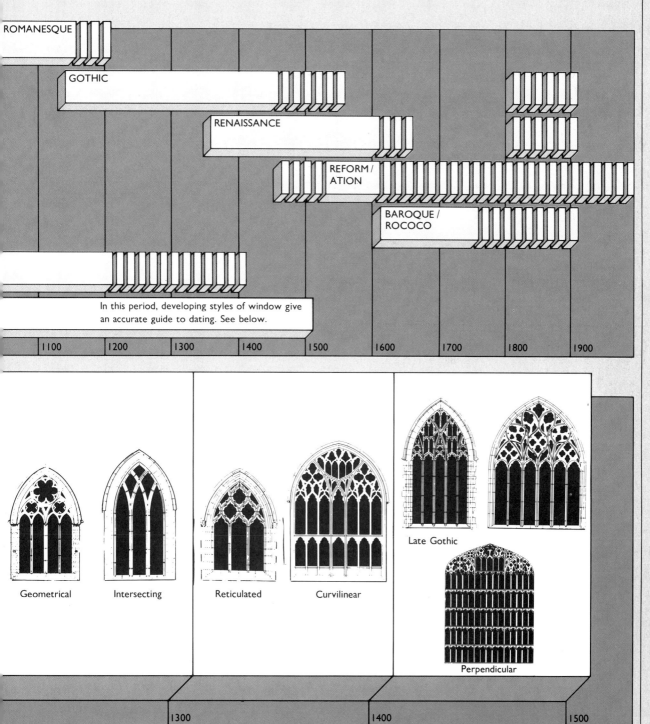

ROMANESQUE

GOTHIC

RENAISSANCE

REFORM / ATION

BAROQUE / ROCOCO

In this period, developing styles of window give an accurate guide to dating. See below.

1100	1200	1300	1400	1500	1600	1700	1800	1900

Geometrical   Intersecting   Reticulated   Curvilinear

Late Gothic

Perpendicular

1300	1400	1500

Arches and Vaults

THIS PAGE, RIGHT. *Sturdy, undecorated round-headed vaults in the crypt of Canterbury Cathedral.* OPPOSITE, LEFT *Gothic vaulting, decorated with delicate ribs and bosses.* RIGHT *Lace-like fan vaulting dates from the English 'Perpendicular' period.*

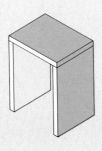

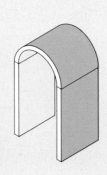

The problem of building doors and windows has been solved in a variety of ways. The structural strength of the building must not be lost because of these openings. The simplest solution is a flat stone or wood lintel which sits on top of the supporting columns.

After the Romanesque period rectangular windows were rare in churches. One reason was strength. The load on a lintel could easily crack it. An arch spreads the thrust and is inherently stronger. The natural strength of arches is such that they often remain in place after surrounding walls have collapsed.

A Romanesque arch is very similar to the arches used by the Romans in their vast building programme. Yet making round-headed arches on a large scale creates problems. The width of the archway is determined by the radius of the arch.

This causes particular problems where a narrow transept meets a wide nave: the different widths of arch have to meet at the same height and so the narrower transept arch has to begin its curvature higher than the nave arch.

The solution to this was the invention of the pointed arch. This enabled a much expanded variety of building forms. Unequal widths of arch can still reach the same height, for the angle of the curve can vary as needed. A pointed arch can be tall or broad and still retain its strength.

The top of the arch can come within a few degrees of horizontal before it becomes weak. This style of flattened or depressed arch was very popular in the sixteenth century English style known as Perpendicular.

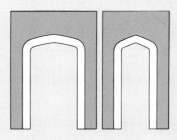

The principles of the arch are true of the vault as well. Vaults are simply a lattice of arches with some kind of infill between the ribs.

Vaults were a fashionable challenge to the architect and because of the expense incurred in their construction they were often built after the basic building was complete.

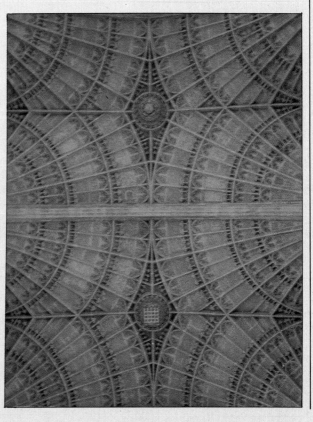

Fittings and Furnishings

By looking at some of the furnishings of the building we can see not only what it is used for, but also what sort of life and beliefs are expressed.

In many churches there has been a centuries-old tradition, dating back to the Old Testament of the Bible, to stress quality, artistry and craftsman-ship: nothing but the best would do for the house of God.

This tended to shift the emphasis, however, from the church as people to the church as a building. So in 'Reformed' churches there was a return to a simpler style, emphasizing the building as a meeting-place rather than 'temple'.

Fonts

The font is used for baptizing people: the children or adults are sprinkled with water as a symbol of the washing away of their sin. In medieval churches the font was almost always positioned near the entrance to the church, symbolizing the entry into the family of God. In Baptist and some other free churches baptism is carried out by 'total immersion'. A baptismal pool at the front of the church is generally covered over when not in use.

ABOVE *An elaborate font cover.* BELOW *Designs drawn from pre-Christian Viking legends.*

Pulpits

The pulpit is the other main focal point: in churches and chapels emphasizing preaching it is often the main one. The teaching and preaching of the 'Word of God', the Bible, was re-instated at the time of the sixteenth-century Reformation, and the centrality of preaching is also reflected in other churches built at a time of revival and renewal.
When the new emphasis on

preaching led to the development of the galleried church, pulpits rose to great heights so the preacher could address the gallery as well as the floor level. Stairs led up to the pulpit, which in some instances was double or treble tiered – the lower levels used for announcement and readings, the uppermost level for preaching. The pulpit was normally placed against one side of the arcade.

Made just after the Reformation, this pulpit is built into the 'box' pews. Above is a sounding board or 'tester'.

Lecterns

The lectern often balances the pulpit on the other side of the nave. From here the service may be conducted, or at least the Bible 'lessons' read; but the preaching is from the pulpit.

Medieval brass pulpits are often in the form of an eagle, with spread wings supporting the Bible.

Choir Screens

Choir screens are often among the more ornate furnishings in the church. In Eastern Orthodox churches, the screens are covered with painted icons – images which are used to focus meditation and worship. By the end of the Middle Ages, with the stress on the 'priestly' function of the clergy and the mass as 'sacrifice' most churches were divided in two, the eastern end for the clergy and the west for the people. The choir screen marked the boundary, emphasizing the mystery of the service in the chancel. The screen had at least one door in the centre for processions to pass through, and was often surmounted by a **rood** – a crucifix attached to a horizontal beam. The choir screen is sometimes referred to as the rood screen. After the Reformation the choir screens were either removed or altered as a demonstration of the Reformers' teaching that all people could have direct access to God through Christ. There was no need for priests or sacrifice. In England the screens unfortunately became the most convenient place to put the organ pipes – in many churches the organ appears as an ungainly intrusion. Many screens were again built in the nineteenth century, with the revival of sacrificial ideas of Communion and the new interest in Gothic architecture.

Choir Stalls

The choir stalls are often the most impressive seating in a church. In monastic churches, the monks would use these tiered walled seats in saying their daily 'offices' – prayers and services said up to seven times a day. As this involved hours of standing in prayer, a narrow shelf-like ledge on the underside of a raised seat provided the monk with something to lean against. Called **misericords,** these props were customarily carved in a whimsical fashion.

In large churches elaborately carved seating was provided for the choir.

Tables/Altars

The communion table or 'altar' is often the focal point of the building. Where it is a simple wooden table this is a reminder of its use as a table for a memorial meal: at the Communion service it is used for the bread and the wine. A stone or marble altar may reflect a belief in the Communion or Mass as re-enactment of the sacrifice of Jesus (see previous section).

BELOW *In this church a modern communion table is placed closer to the congregation than the old one.*

Pews

Pews are today a dominant feature in many church buildings. It was not common to sit in church until the fifteenth century. At first the weary and laden had to bring their own chairs, but eventually the more far-sighted churches decided that it would be easier to provide seating. With the Reformation came the first regular appearance of pews is in Protestant churches, when preaching became the central component of the service. Seats were arranged in a semi-circle around the pulpit. Later they were fixed to the floor. By the eighteenth century pews were often 'sold' to families in the community. In some instances they were considered private property and decorated according to the owner's (sometimes peculiar) taste. In some churches there are box pews which date from this time, these were occasionally equipped with padded armchairs and fireplaces!

Wooden pews, in this case 'box' pews, traditionally provide seating for the congregation. However, their arrangement is inflexible, so some churches now prefer chairs.

Confessionals

Confessionals or confession boxes are common in most Roman Catholic churches. The priest sits to listen to those who make their confession. The box serves the purpose of focussing attention on the words of the priest rather than on his person. Confessionals usually have a small window or aperture to speak through.

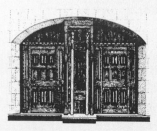

Candles

Candles begin to appear after about AD 1100. Gigantic candlesticks in some churches show the difficulty of trying to illuminate them by candlelight! Special lighters and snuffers soon followed.

Memorial Tombs

Memorial tombs are a feature of many old church buildings. The early church's practice of burying the more famous or influential within the church building continued until the present century. The monuments, shrines and plaques in churches make an illuminating study in themselves. The various stages of church patronage can often be worked out. In some cases the monuments themselves came to be the church's most important asset.

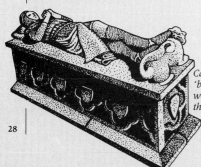

Carved stone tombs and decorated 'brasses' mark the place where wealthy or prominent members of the community were buried.

PART 2
THE STORY OF
CHURCH BUILDING

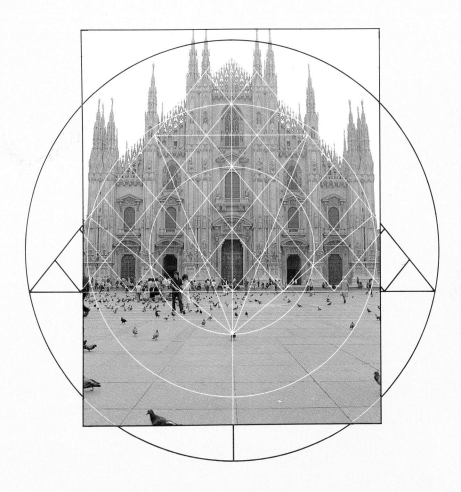

The last great medieval Gothic
cathedral was built in Milan,
Italy. Its entire construction was
based on an elaborate geometrical
grid of intersecting circles and
equilateral triangles, which
had a metaphysical meaning
as well as a satisfying form.

29

The First Christians

In Jerusalem in the year 30AD, Jesus of Nazareth was crucified and his followers fled in despair. Three days later their lives had changed: Jesus had been raised to new life. As the weeks went by, they came to understand what this meant, and at last, Jesus left them for the final time. What were the disciples to do now? Jesus had told them that they were to go into all the world to spread the good news of new life – but first they were to wait for him to send them his Holy Spirit. Ten days later, on the feast of Pentecost, the Spirit came. This was the explosive birth of the Christian church.

As the first Christians were predominantly Jewish, the natural place to meet was the Temple or synagogue. The Temple in Jerusalem was an impressive building, the religious centre of Judaism, but it was not the right building for the new faith. The Christians believed that the daily ritual of sacrifice, the central part of Jewish ceremony, was no longer necessary. The death of Jesus on the cross was a once-for-all sacrifice for human sin.

A better 'model' for the Christian gatherings was the Jewish synagogue. The synagogue had been developed to maintain the Jewish faith when the Jews were in exile. By this time it had become the meeting-place of the local community.

The tension between the idea of a church-building as 'temple', to re-enact the sacrifice of Jesus, or simply as 'meeting-place', has remained with the Christian churches since those early days. As the story unfolds, as we shall see, different groups have emphasized one side or the other, with profound implications for the style and architecture of the buildings they have used.

At the heart of the Christian faith is the belief that Christ's followers belong together. Early references to the Christians often mention their communal life and support. At first the common meeting-place was the home, and because the primary part of Christian worship was the celebration of the Lord's Supper, or Eucharist ('thanksgiving'), most of their meetings were held in the dining-room.

Houses in Palestine often had three or four stories and the dining-room was usually on the top floor (hence the 'upper room' described in the Gospels where the Last Supper took place). Christians would come together for an ordinary meal, probably prepared by the women of the group. Sitting around a large table on couches or benches the congregation would exchange news, study and pray together and review the work they were involved in. The supper would be concluded with a communal sharing of bread and wine in remembrance of Christ's death.

A meeting like this took place at Troas once, when the apostle Paul was the special guest. The book of Acts records how, during the long meeting in a crowded room, a young man perched on the windowsill literally dropped off!

Other meeting-places would be determined by circumstances or planning. Informal public meetings in the market-place might be organized for preaching. Meetings in the Temple precincts might be arranged to continue the dialogue with the Jews about who Jesus was. For a special visitor a large hall might be hired to accommodate the extra numbers, as when Paul spoke at Ephesus.

Small groups of Christians sprang up in the cities throughout Asia Minor and grew to become sizable communities. Because of the restrictions on domestic space, large churches often would be spread between homes. The first 'purpose-built' church buildings were generally similar to ordinary houses. Inside, the rooms equivalent to sleeping and living quarters would have been used as classrooms and for storing the

Jerusalem was the spring-board of the Christian faith. In the first century it was dominated by the Temple, centre of the Jewish sacrificial system. In AD 70 this was destroyed by the Romans. The new Christians needed not a temple, for Jesus had died as a once-for-all sacrifice for sin, but a meeting-place. Their model was not the Temple but the Jewish synogogue.

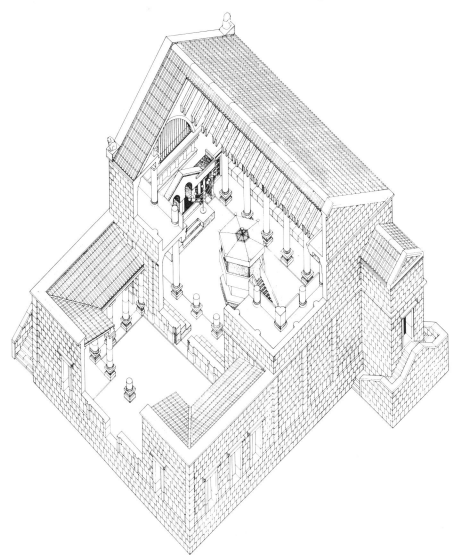

goods which were distributed to the poor. The large upper room would still have been the assembly areas.

The Christian population continued to swell in the second and third centuries. By the year 250 two-thirds of Asia Minor was Christian, and in Rome the community numbered between thirty and fifty thousand. Although the house-church would still have been an important place for worship, larger church buildings were constructed, patterned on the usual form for large halls, the basilica.

But building churches was not simple. Not only was there Roman red tape and crushing taxation, there was also constant uncertainty about the attitude of the Roman state to the church. The political wind could change overnight.

To begin with, the Roman Empire regarded the Christians as a Jewish sect.

They did not much care what people believed so long as they paid their taxes and treated officials with respect. But by the end of the first century the Eastern idea of ruler-worship had been imported to Rome. When it was applied as a test of loyalty to the regime, the Christians usually refused to venerate the emperor. Often this led to persecution and church property was confiscated or destroyed.

Yet the church continued to grow. Even the Roman persecutors were impressed with the Christians' fortitude in the face of torture and death. The tribulations may have dispersed the church, but far from destroying it, they toughened it. And as Christianity became more acceptable it attracted people in prominent positions, until eventually it was even adopted by its former enemy – the Roman Emperor.

The meeting-place for every Jewish community was the local synagogue. It was a simple hall with seats and a raised reading desk. Next to it there might be a room used as school or library.

The Official Church

The Emperor Constantine was converted to Christianity by a vision. He was instructed to put the sign of the cross on his soldiers' uniforms before a crucial battle. When the battle was won Constantine became the first powerful political leader to embrace Christianity.

Now, in the Edict of Milan in 313, the faith was recognized and granted official status. Though Constantine himself was not baptized until he was on his death-bed, he regarded himself as the thirteenth apostle, God's appointed 'vicar'. He asserted himself in church affairs by mediating in doctrinal disputes and presiding over church councils and he applied the leverage of the state to ensure that the decisions of those councils were upheld.

State patronage changed almost everything in the church. Simple house-groups gave way to larger congregations managed by full-time professional clergy. The participation of ordinary 'lay' people decreased, and ceremony became more pronounced in church services. Bishops and other church 'officials' took to wearing insignia of rank on their vestments in imitation of the status symbols of the imperial court.

These changes in the social profile of the church naturally affected church building. The domestic model was no longer adequate to accommodate the expanding needs of both clergy and congregation. One end of the church became the seat of the clergy, who were separated from the people by means of a screen and a raised floor. The simple wooden communion table was replaced by a more substantial and ornate one, becoming an altar, sometimes covered with precious metals and jewels.

Now that the dignity of the church was assured by imperial patronage, there was demand for buildings of the highest order. The model for these came from the architectural forms of public buildings – palaces, forums and temples. Yet it was clear to Christians that the pagan religious architecture of antiquity was not a suitable pattern. Temples in particular had unsavoury associations. Also the form was impractical, for temples were designed as a place for individuals to adore an image, not for large congregations to meet together.

So it was the official state architecture which was adopted. The most common form of public building was the basilica. In its simplest form this was a long timber-roofed hall ending in a semi-circular 'apse', with windows in the side walls. Such buildings could serve a variety of functions: audience hall, trading market, banquet hall, imperial forum.

Groups of Christians adapted the basilica to meet their own special needs or the wishes of a patron. Christianity was now socially acceptable, so there were funds enough for construction. Differences came from circumstances; a commemorative chapel sponsored by a wealthy patron would be more lavish and intimate than a basilica designed for a congregation of five thousand. Because there was no precedent for public church building, a great variety of experimental forms appeared.

Many small chapels were built as monuments to martyrs because of the growing veneration of those who had died under persecution. The 'martyria' often acquired porches, wings and rooms to accommodate those who wished to be buried near the martyr – almost as a superstitious way of guaranteeing salvation. Many of these memorials gradually became churches for the local community, and often required further rebuilding. This has been a common process: some Italian churches today are built on sites known to have been occupied by at least a dozen previous buildings.

Other churches were purpose-built to honour a saint or martyr and to accommodate a congregation. The old St Peter's basilica in Rome (replaced by the present building in the sixteenth century) was designed with a large 'transept' (or 'cross-piece') at the east end to permit pilgrims to circulate in front of the shrine. There was no seating. The service was conducted with the whole of the large congregation standing. Celebration of the Eucharist, the Mass, became a dramatic re-enactment of Christ's sacrifice: the action was now round the altar, and worshippers would be able to move around to view the pattern of service, the liturgy, more clearly.

By the end of the fifth century it was common to orientate churches so that as one faced the altar one was also facing east – toward Jerusalem. This became required

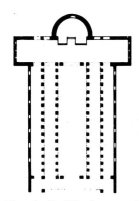

The style of building known as the basilica was common amongst wealthy Romans. Big basilicas were very suitable for larger Christian groups; there was plenty of space for the congregation and a natural focal point for ministers leading the service.

practice by the Middle Ages.

As the church consolidated its power, in Europe a more uniform architectural policy resulted. The nave and aisles of the early basilica developed into the classic form of the medieval cathedral. The pattern of service, the liturgy, influenced by the manners of the imperial court, was handed down to the medieval church.

The early alliance of the church and state clearly assisted the spread of Christianity. But the very expansion of the church's power brought difficulties with it. Some Christians were greatly alarmed by the

indentification with secular powers, particularly when emperors made decisions about church doctrine. The elevated position of secular rulers in the church hierarchy was intended to reflect the cooperation of a Christian society, but more often led to power struggles. The question of the nature of the church's authority in society was to become one of the recurring themes of medieval history.

THE BASILICA

The basilica of Santa Sabina in Rome is remarkably well preserved. It gives a good idea of the spacious interior, decorated simply with patterning on the marble surfaces.

The original form of the basilica was a long shoe-box-shaped building.

The interior of the building was generally brighter than secular basilicas and was often decorated with paintings of Christian symbols, geometric designs, words from the Bible and creeds.

②

The form of service (or 'liturgy') varied. The elders or clergy might be seated in front of the altar table or behind it. The bishop's throne or cathedra might be raised on a platform. An extension of this platform into the nave called an ambo would serve as a place for the reading of lessons.

①

The timber roof was supported by two internal rows of columns.

Secondary lowered roofs often covered the aisles and had windows above them onto the central nave.

③

The eastern end of the building, where the service was conducted, was usually rounded into an apse.

⑤

Those under instruction for baptism ('catechumens') had a separate building or a foyer-like division in the west part of the church.

④

The side aisle and a clear space in front of the apse were used for processions, and so came to be known as the ambulatory.

The Eastern Church

Over the centuries the Eastern Church has developed separately from the West. In the Soviet Union the Russian Orthodox church is active (BELOW). *In Greece there are tens of thousands of tiny chapels* (OPPOSITE).

While the churches near Rome naturally developed the Roman style of building, the basilica, in the Eastern part of the Roman Empire rather different needs and emphases were developing. The great city on the Bosphorus, Constantinople (now Istanbul) became the centre of the Eastern Orthodox faith which continues its own traditions to this day.

The Eastern Church placed great stress on symbol and ritual. The clergy dominated the liturgy even more than in the West: services became priestly actions carried out on behalf of the people. The ritual celebration of the Eucharist was carried out in a 'chancel', a holy of holies separated from the gaze of the common people by screens.

The nave had become the place of the congregation in churches in the West: in the East the people were squeezed out still further, as the nave was used for processions and the congregation was relegated to the side aisles.

The solemn performance of the Eucharist in the East did not easily fit into the limits imposed by the basilica type of building. The basilica has no natural centre. A new type of building was required to accommodate the shift in doctrinal viewpoint.

One particularly well-known church reflects this new emphasis: Saint Sophia in Constantinople. Now an Islamic mosque, it was built by the Emperor Justinian in the early sixth century at staggering cost. Tradition has it that on the day of the church's consecration, referring to the Jewish Temple, Justinian exclaimed, 'Solomon, I have surpassed you!'

The centrality of the ritual was reflected in a central-plan building covered by a massive dome. The technical challenge required architects versed in structural dynamics, physics and mathematics. The dome had to be light enough to be carried by the walls, yet resilient enough to withstand the stresses of wind, weather and earthquake. Placing a dome on a square obviously limits the points of attachment, so it was necessary to design 'squinches' for the corners to distribute the weight evenly, so giving the interior of the building its characteristic octagonal shape.

The resulting building is enormous: full of mystery yet light and airy. Solid masses are made soft by tinted stone, cut and polished to show its patterned 'figure'. Silver, gold and acres of mosaics splinter the light from the windows in the rim of the dome and create a resonant sense of mystery. It is easy to imagine how the mystery of the building would have been heightened during its use. The congregation in the side aisles only catch glimpses of the processions. First comes the bishop in his robes, followed by the clergy bearing the bread and wine to the altar. Light from the dome falls in long rays in the mixture of

dust and the smoke of incense. The procession halts, then to the sound of bells and Greek chants slowly passes through the altar screen to the sanctuary beyond. The actual celebration of the Eucharist takes place out of sight in the screened-off chancel.

The rituals that were visible often were those reflecting the belief that the Emperor and the Patriarch were representatives of 'the halves of God'. Their ritual 'kiss of peace' under the great dome was a symbol of the religious and secular cooperation in the Christian state. This fusion of politics, theology and acting is difficult for us to grasp. For the man of the sixth century, the church building was a model of heaven on earth, a kind of preview of the presence of God in the company of the saints. The

clergy were the entrusted agents of communication with God. The radiance of the gilded dome of the church was a reminder to all in the city of the power of God and his representatives, and of the fact that God's ways can never be fully understood by men.

The mystical conception of Christian worship points toward the undefinable character of God's majesty. In the architecture of the Eastern church there is a pervading sense of those words the Bible uses to describe God - light, breath, and fire.

Often plain outside, Greek Orthodox churches are richly decorated inside – reflecting the fact that God is not simply concerned with external appearances. The atmosphere inside is also a reminder of the splendour and mystery of God. Often icons – images of saints – are used as an aid to worship.

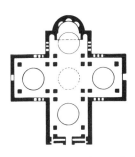

Many Eastern churches are built on the plan of the 'Greek cross', with four arms of equal length.

Commissioned by the Emperor Justinian as the greatest church of the Byzantine Empire, Santa Sophia in present-day Istanbul, Turkey, was the most ambitious building that had ever been undertaken. When the Turks took Constantinople in 1453 they turned it into a mosque, but even though they whitewashed over the mosaics and put up Islamic texts, the building still maintains much of its glory and mystery.

THE ART OF MOSAICS

Apart from the shape of the building, the most obvious innovation in the East was the splendour of the mosaics and other decoration. Some of the finest are to be seen in a city which lay on the border of the Eastern and Western Empires, the Aegean coast town of Ravenna in Italy.

Though the ground-plans in Ravenna are still mainly of the Roman basilica type, the decoration of the buildings from the fifth and sixth century is Eastern. Built for the imperial court when it had to remove from Rome in the fifth century because of barbarian invasions, most of the dozen buildings have been scarcely altered since their construction. In S. Apollinare Nuovo, for instance, the lavish decoration transforms the piers and walls by an infusion of colour, making the large areas of stonework 'melt away'. There are horizontal bands of contrasting masonry, and the light filtering in illuminates the rich texture of the incized capitals and glittering mosaics.

The decorations are not just wallpaper. They reflect the meaning of the church and the history of God's acts of salvation. Kings, elders, prophets and saints are a reminder of the past and an aid to reflection and meditation.

This gold mosaic from the church of San Vitale in Ravenna is a portrait of the emperor Justinian who commissioned the building.

37

Christian Communities: the Monasteries

It was around the year 300 that groups of Christians in Egypt first set up communities 'away from the world' where they could live out in rigorous asceticism the demands of piety and self-denial. The remote monastery of St Catherine (OPPOSITE) at the foot of Mount Sinai was begun in the sixth century.

Other groups of monks live in greater contact with the outside world, in service and worship.

For all its splendour and status, the secularized church of Constantine's empire repelled some Christians because of its pomp and worldliness. Many of the dissatisfied joined monsteries – communities devoted to the disciplines of study, work and regular prayer. When barbarian invasions upset the secular foundations of the official church it was the monasteries which proved most hardy. Located in remote and often inhospitable places, the monasteries lived out the dark ages like seed pods awaiting a change in climate.

With Islamic invaders threatening Europe from the south and barbarian raiders attacking from the north, there were few places which afforded security. Many sought refuge in the desert. In the sixth and seventh centuries groups of monks left the Mediterranean by boat for the rugged coasts of Cornwall, Ireland or the Hebrides. Using dry stone-wall construction, the immigrant scholars built tiny fortress-like churches. Eventually these coastal monasteries so grew in size and strength that they sponsored missionaries to Britain, and took over the running of the Irish church from the bishops. The Irish church, perched on the edge of the known world, survived with vigour. For churches on the European continent, the climate was harsh until the ninth century when the migrations had slowed down and a greater political stability permitted the growth of monasticism.

The Italian monk Benedict was to become the most influential designer of patterns of monastic life. He upgraded the image of the monk and paved the way to the belief that gifts to monks were 'damnation-deductible'. As a result, land-owners, knights and princes liberally endowed the monasteries. They became formidable institutions. Eventually the rigours of vows became incompatible with the extravagence of financial management. The history of monasticism is a constant pendulum swing from reform to excess.

Contemplation, the disciplined attitude to work and (in most orders) access to books helped the monasteries develop the arts. The monastery of Cluny, founded in the tenth century, became for a time the artistic centre of Europe. It is not unreasonable to suppose that the architecture of the great abbey was the product of the minds of monks if not their hands. As Cluny grew in power and fostered satellite monasteries, its artisans and style spread too. Cluny supported pilgrimages and so its influence led to the construction of similarly-styled monasteries right along the pilgrim routes.

Monastery churches were commonly built in the form of basilicas with a number of transepts, often with towers. Because an active monastery would have over 400 monks, a great deal of space was required for them to say their daily offices, the seven set liturgies. If a monastic church did not also serve a local secular community, choir stalls might fill the entire nave – indeed some churches were constructed without naves. Theoretically, decoration was sparse. But St Bernard, the most famous of all medieval monks, had Cluny itself in mind when he asked other monks, 'Tell me, you professors of Poverty, what is gold doing in a holy place?'

The construction of monastic churches in remote locations taxed the skill and imagination of the builders. Built on mountain tops, into cliff faces or in the desolate emptiness of the wilderness, the structures posed immense logistical problems.

After the Reformation, the ascetic life lost much of its popularity and many monastic foundations were converted for other uses. New orders continued to be instituted until well into the nineteenth century, but the scale of monastic building never again equalled the scope of the eleventh and twelfth centuries.

Down the centuries, monasteries have been important centres of learning, teaching, medical work, missionary outreach and cultural life. Santo Domingo de Silos in Spain (RIGHT) *dates from the eleventh century. Its peaceful cloisters are decorated with delicate sculpture of New Testament stories.*

Foundations of Western Society: Romanesque

The development of the Romanesque style between about 1050 and 1200 has long puzzled historians. Buildings of this period all over Europe show a remarkable similarity – but no clear source. The term 'Romanesque' indicates the most obvious influence: late Roman building. Roman ruins abound in Europe today and there would have been many more in the eleventh century, but why would church builders suddenly begin to copy Roman architecture?

Close inspection of Romanesque architecture reveals many 'un-Roman' details - rugged 'chevron' ornament, fantastic carved figures and patterning which is almost like calligraphy. Scholars have traced some of these elements to Byzantine, Islamic and Celtic sources, an indication of the importance of medieval trade and pilgrimage routes.

One key factor leading to the upsurge of building in the eleventh century was the fact that the world had not ended! Christians believe that Christ will return to earth to bring this world to its conclusion. There had been a widespread belief that this

The five centuries following Rome's collapse in AD 476 gave rise to hardly any sizeable building in Europe except in the reign of the emperor Charlemagne. The chapel of his great palace at Aachen, Germany, (Aix-la-Chapelle) still stands. Octagonal in plan, it is built in Roman style.

In England, stone churches were built to replace former wooden buildings which have not survived. Windows were small (ABOVE), giving very sombre interiors (BELOW).

Even with their tall columns and more spacious interiors (OPPOSITE), churches of the Romanesque period were still dark. Extraordinary carving, for example at Souillac in France (INSERT), was common.

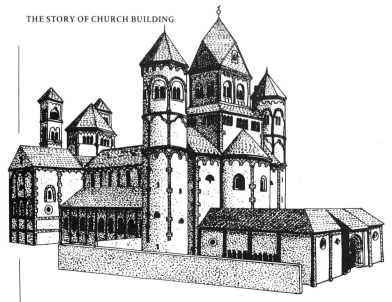

'Second Coming' would be in the year 1000.
When Christ did not return, it was as if
people waited for a while and then got back
to work. By the mid-eleventh century a new
enthusiasm for building had replaced the
preparations for the Second Coming. Trade,
commerce and pilgrimage blossomed. Cities
sprang up along the busiest commercial
thoroughfares. At the same time, new
monasteries were set up along the trade
routes. At first simple retreats, they became
influential power-centres, wealthy enough
to support lavish building programmes.
Churches of hewn stone replaced wooden
ones. They were larger, longer and more
complex structures, many with timber or
stone spires. Such churches would have
been the most prominent buildings in the
community, for virtually all domestic
buildings were built of timber. So the local
church was a matter of considerable civic
pride. It was a landmark which could be
seen from afar, and a cultural marvel to be
examined at close range. On Sundays the
whole town would meet there and a fair
volume of trade would be conducted
around it through the week.

Romanesque churches display a
delightful variety of regional detail. In their
basic structure and form, however, all are
very similar. They are really modified
basilicas. The main change was to the roof:
timber roofs were replaced by tunnel vaults
of massive masonry. Eventually the 'rib
vault' – crossed semi-circular arches of stone
spanning the nave – was developed. Stone
ribs are stronger and more fire-resistant
than timber, but far more complex to
construct. Each stone had to be precisely
cut. Timber forms called 'centering' held
the stones in place until the mortar set. The
spaces between the ribs were then filled in
with a mixture of mortar and rubble on a
woven lattice of willow branches. Later,

OPPOSITE *Romanesque churches in Germany are sturdy and solid, often with several towers. The monastery church of Maria Laach (ABOVE) and the cathedral at Speyer are typical. Inside, too, such as Mainz (BELOW), they are simple and dark.*

Across Europe, styles and details were similar, whether in a French cathedral (Poitiers, BELOW) or an English parish church (Stewkley, RIGHT). English architecture of the period is known as Norman, since it was the Norman conquerors who brought it with them from France.

vaults were built entirely from stone.

The extra weight of the ribbed vault and the stone walls of the nave meant that the arcade, aisle walls and buttressing had to be stronger. To the eleventh-century builder strength meant mass. Columns in Romanesque churches sometimes have the girth of a small elephant and walls often spread to fifteen feet thick. Round-headed

Sweden has some delightful variants of Romanesque building at Vitaby (ABOVE) and Hagby (BELOW). Dalby (RIGHT) is the oldest stone church in the country.

arches linked the arcade to the aisle, and the windows echoed the shape. The weight, the simplicity of form and the logic of this system make these churches very attractive to us today (though to the Gothic architect they seemed 'childish'). The earliest Romanesque churches make up for any elegance they may lack by their great, solemn strength. The forms were extensively copied in the Romantic revival of the nineteenth century.

It was natural that changes occurred quickly in such an intensive period of building. The rough-and-ready masonry of the early Romanesque churches was soon replaced with more sophisticated work.

Later, columns were made of cylindrical blocks rather than stones laid like brick.

More complex elevations evolved. 'Blind arcading' emphasized the wall surfaces and linked the bays together.

Eventually the massive single column in the nave arcade gave way to the 'compound pier', a cluster of shafts bearing several different directions of thrust together at one strategic point.

The ground-plan of these churches anticipate the Gothic plans, with staggered apses, ambulatories and radiating chapels.

The nave bays are usually square in plan, and the aisles together take a quarter of the total width. These dimensions were determined by the restrictions of round arches. The outside of the church reflected the interior structure. Simple buttresses divided the side into bays and 'blind arcading' was the principle form of ornament.

One Romanesque invention was the twin western facade; an idea which was developed by the Gothic builders and has become the norm for church building ever since.

Perhaps the most notable legacy of the

Romanesque is its carving. Scenes on columns in the nave and cloisters were visual aids, with a dramatic scene around every corner. The artistic fashion of our own age makes us look at these rugged carvings as 'art' rather than as the lessons they were intended to be. Geometric carving was very popular, judging by the frequency of its appearance. Dog-tooth, chevron, ball-and-dagger, diaper, running dog – these are some of the names given to recurring designs; but many sculptors simply produced their own designs.

The riot of sculpture on the west front was intended to be an advertisement for the church and also a reminder of the seriousness of life. A common arrangement is that the major virtues and vices are portrayed on either side, with Christ on the Throne of Judgement between them. Considerable imagination goes into depicting the fate of the wicked. The society of the time was based on feudalism, with its underlying notions of obligation, duty, punishment and reward. So people readily believed that God 'kept score' just as they did. The sculpture on the front of the local church was an ever-present reminder of the

The doorway of Kilpeck church in the west of England (ABOVE) shows how local sculptors mingled Romanesque styles with local influences.

Churches on pilgrim routes in France are very large, with chapels around the apse so that pilgrims could see local relics.

The church of St Servatius in Maastricht, Holland, is built on the site of a sixth-century chapel. The Romanesque west end has been added to, over the centuries: the towers date from the nineteenth century.

Romanesque churches were built by itinerant craftsmen who took their designs with them. So there is an extraordinary similarity of style right across Europe. These three carvings showing Christ in glory come from church doorways in Moissac, France (RIGHT), *Barfreston, England* (ABOVE) *and Soria, Spain* (BELOW).

stakes of life, and of the need for the church, though the more basic Christian gospel of free forgiveness for the sinner was less clear.

The eleventh century marks the beginning of an all-embracing society. The church's authority and teaching extended beyond national boundaries. The solidity and imagination of Romanesque architecture reflects both the seriousness with which the church was viewed and also the magical world which medieval man saw all around him.

THE ART
OF THE SCULPTOR

The earliest church buildings were quite plain. A community struggling to survive has little time for ornament and decoration. Image worship in surrounding pagan cultures also made some Christians strongly against religious sculpture at all.

As the church grew in size and power many members wanted to make the place of worship more prominent and more fitting. God is a God of beauty, they reasoned, and sculptural decoration can be used to express faith.

The use of sculpture in church architecture began to flourish in the Romanesque period. At first decoration consisted mainly of incised geometric patterns and floral ornaments, but the human figure (which has always attracted the artist) and other figurative sculpture followed. To illiterate people statuary and narrative scenes were a visual reminder of the serious truths of the Christian life.

Most of the Romanesque carving is not very naturalistic. By our standards their human forms are crude and stylized. But for the Romanesque artist and his patron these rough and ready figures rightly placed the emphasis of the carvings on the scene rather than the individual characters. Many of these carvings have an undeniable power, far in excess of smoother, more tastefully proportioned carvings from some later periods.

In Gothic art sculpture becomes more important in its own right. Figures are given a greater sense of weight and posture. They look at one another and gesture to the viewer with real feeling. The relationship between the sculptural groupings and the architecture as a whole also becomes more important. By the twelfth century sculpture was considered an essential part of a church and elaborate treatises were compiled about the proper arrangement of figures for each different part of the church.

Carvers working their way along the trade and pilgrim routes saw the work of other sculptors and engaged in a fruitful collaboration with other builders and masons. We know little of their actual working methods. There is some reference to the use of models, but the greatest emphasis seems to have been on theory. There were many attempts to discern underlying geometrical principles governing the human figure. Certain proportions were considered harmonious, and a vast lore of symbolic imagery was built up. Yet artists flexed these rules as much as they discussed them.

English sculpture in the Romanesque period was not as fine as French. Nonetheless, the work

In the fanciful details of many capitals and corbels we can see that the imaginative life of the sculptor was very rich.

Sculpture must have proved very popular, for in some churches it is hard to see the building for the decoration. In medieval English churches the west front is often wider than the building itself – making a

of some craftsmen was superb. This carving of six of the apostles is in the porch of Malmesbury Abbey.

kind of backdrop, much like that of the altar screen. This permitted a fuller display of statuary of biblical figures and saints (commonly painted in bright colours). In the cathedral at Wells, for example, the screen is so large that the doors scarcely rise above the level of the pediment. In France, by contrast, the doorways are much larger, with doorway arches often rising nearly to the full height of the church, and with many rows of statues carved into the moulding of the arch. The columns supporting the arch are often reserved for particularly notable figures – the archangel Michael or the apostle Peter standing guard with his set of keys.

The sculpture of west fronts is a study in itself. Romanesque churches tend to be covered with a writhing mass of people and mythical creatures with isolated clusters of the godly holding them at bay. The technical ability of the best of these carvings ranks them as important reference points for modern sculptors. Certainly the majestic pose of the 'kings' in the Chartres portal suggests an artist of sensitive humanity as well as commanding skill.

In modern churches taste and economics have severely curtailed the use of sculpture. There may be a few plaques or a small scene, but the modern world itself provides so much imagery through the media that sculptural portrayals have rather fallen into disfavour. Newer abstract experiments have not yet achieved the same universal language as sculpture did in the medieval world, and probably never will. Yet the attraction of carved things remains strong, and perhaps a greater use of sculpture in churches may be developed in the future.

Sculptors included charming detail in their work, even at points which are hardly visible to the human eye; this angel is from the cathedral at Rheims, France.

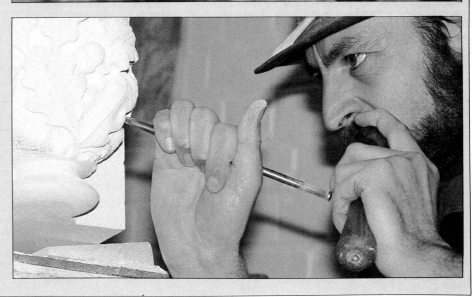

BELOW *Today sculptors are kept busy restoring old buildings.*

49

Pilgrims and Pilgrimage

Since the fourth century, the Holy Land has been a major destination for pilgrims. Sizeable churches have been built on the sites of Biblical events, for example the Church of the Nativity in Bethlehem.

The 'sites' of Christendom attract visitors by the tens of thousands today. Yet few modern tourists would think of spending two or three years on foot to reach their destination; fewer still would travel without money, maps or hotel reservations – all in the hope of ensuring salvation. But this was common in the eleventh and twelfth centuries.

It is hard to fathom the phenomenal magnetism the holy sites held. What we see is a host of churches which were important pilgrim sites, and a few seemingly superstitious objects which apparently made all the deprivation and hardship of pilgrimage worthwhile. The relics were of extraordinary importance. Without them there would have been no pilgrim routes, and probably no crusades either. Churches sprang up all along the pilgrimage roads, and it was those which had important relics which became the major stopping points.

There were three primary pilgrimage routes in the Middle Ages: to Jerusalem, to Rome and to Santiago de Compostella in Spain. Jerusalem was an important city for obvious reasons, for, as one early pilgrim wrote, what could be better than 'to put the finishing touch to virtue by adoring Christ in the very place where the gospel first shone forth from the cross'. Travellers could visit the Church of the Nativity, the Church of the Holy Sepulchre, see the place where Christ was put on trial before Pilate and revere countless relics. This was an

The long business of pilgrimage was for some an entertaining social event as well as a spiritual exercise.

expensive and time-consuming journey (up to seven years), made even more difficult since Palestine was occupied by the Moorish 'infidel'. Pilgrims to Jerusalem often travelled in armed bands; some of these journeys were little different from crusades.

Rome was important for two reasons. It was the seat of the Western church, and it was steeped in the history of the martyrs. It became customary for newly-appointed bishops to make the pilgrimage to Rome. A certain degree of confusion between ancient Roman statues and memorials to Christian martyrs added to the impression of the Christian heritage of the city. The most important relics of the pilgrimage to Rome were held in the Lateran Basilica; they were the heads of the apostles Peter and Paul. The church also exhibited the ark of the covenant, the tablets on which Moses wrote the ten commandments, the rod of Moses' brother Aaron, an urn of manna, John the Baptist's hair shirt, the five loaves and two fishes, and the dining table used at the Last Supper!

Despite this impressive catalogue, the most popular route was not to Rome, but to Spain, to Santiago de Compostella and the remains of the apostle James. At the peak of his popularity more than half-a-million pilgrims made the tiring trek over the Pyrenees to Santiago every year. They came primarily from France, but also from England, Germany, and Italy. Not all were devout volunteers seeking spiritual improvement. Many walked the road as punishment. Pilgrimage was prescribed as a means of penance. It was also a convenient way to banish trouble-makers; in thirteenth-century England, for example, the penalty for killing a relative was to go on pilgrimage in chains until they wore off!

The five major routes to Spain were dotted with churches, monasteries and hostels for the pilgrim. Among them are some of the most exquisite churches ever built. Vézelay on its commanding yet serene hilltop site was a marvel then and still is today. Poitiers, with one of the liveliest west fronts in France; Aulnay, with a carved portal showing the influence of Moorish artists, and Le Puy, where the whole church is somewhat Arabic; St Sernin at Toulouse with its immense interior . . . these are only a few. Thousands of architectural remains attest the vitality of the period, and any traveller in France will see them, restored, or in odd new uses: incorporated into the side of a barn or as a bicycle repair shop!

The major pilgrim churches all have a similar architectural form. All are spacious, with a long nave, aisles and gallery. All have wide transepts to hold the crowd of pilgrims and chapels to house the relics. The churches could get very crowded, particularly near the time of St James's day on 25 July. As a contemporary account said, 'No one among the countless thousands of people because of their very destiny could move a foot. No one could do anything but stand like a marble statue, stay benumbed, or, as a last resort, scream . . . The brethren, who were showing the tokens to the visitors . . . having no place to turn, escaped with the relics through the window.'

Some of the later pilgrim churches were designed with practicality in mind. The floor of Chartres cathedral is gently sloped and gutters round the walls allowed the floor to be washed after the crowds had left. The windows were designed to unlatch so that the building could be aired.

The pilgrim routes were important links in a primitive system of communications, and it is not surprising to find that they served as channels for architectural styles. French churches along the route to Spain show many Islamic details such as horseshoe arches and decorative arabesques, which came from Spain.

The tremendous flurry of building along the pilgrim routes in the twelfth century gradually subsided. Festivities and commerce began to obscure any spiritual goals. The Renaissance and the Reformation then undermined the pilgrim spirit. But pilgrimages continued until well into the eighteenth century.

Perhaps the most striking observation to make today is that the art and architecture of the period was thoroughly integrated. The sculpture of the portals, capitals and screens was part of an all-embracing scheme aimed to encourage and teach the traveller. There are different styles and different artistic treatments sometimes drawing on local folklore, but they all tell the same stories. The artist and architect were in no doubt about what their work should communicate.

Tombs of martyrs have been popular pilgrim sites. At Canterbury, pilgrims visited the shrine of Thomas à Becket who was assassinated in 1170 after refusing to allow the state to limit the church's action.

The church of Sainte Foy at Conques in south-west France is typical of churches on the pilgrimage routes to Santiago de Compostella in Spain.

RELICS

The lists of relics are both fascinating and macabre: Peter's tooth, the blood of Jesus, a piece of the head of John the Baptist, bones of Mary Magdalen, a finger of the apostle Thomas, a phial of Mary's milk . . . and all of these were part of one church's collection!

The natural liking for souvenirs and superstition are two of the reasons behind the medieval fascination with religious relics. Originally intended as an aid to devotion, the relics soon seem to have been worshipped in their own right. They were traded, collected, taken on tour. People took oaths on them, and built churches over them.

RIGHT *Relics were often stored in ornate cases which themselves became the object of veneration.*

BELOW *St Ambrose was the influential adviser of Emperor Theodosius in the fourth century. After his death his body was put in a specially-built basilica in Milan, where he had been bishop.*

S. AMBROGIO VESCOVO
(Patrono della Città)
340 - 397

S. GERVASIO e S. PROTASIO
Martiri del secolo I°

It was Helena, mother of the Emperor Constantine, who first actually hunted for relics. Visiting the Holy Land in 326 at the age of sixty-nine she unearthed what she believed to be Christ's cross. This she shipped back to Constantinople. From there over the years it was disseminated in splinters as gifts to the worthy.

By the eleventh century overt worship of relics was commonplace. The church taught that the martyr's example of sacrifice should be followed by the faithful, and therefore took great stock in relics as visual aids. The crusades swelled the number of these mementos in currency.

There is no doubt that virtually all of these relics were spurious – either intentional swindles or innocent mistakes. Cynics have speculated that

there are enough relics of 'the true cross' to construct the Spanish Armada! But notions of 'truth' in the Middle Ages were vastly different from our own bias for empirical 'proof'. The relics were considered 'true' because they had the power to aid worship, even to bring healing, and above all to provide an emotional insurance policy.

They were certainly powerful. The relic bones of St Foy were acquired by the monastery of Conques in France by outright theft. A monk infiltrated the neighbouring monastery at Agen and waited ten years for his chance to make off with them in the night. Conques quickly shot to prominence and Agen folded.

Such was the worth of relics that complex procedures were

devised to safeguard them. Workmen excavating the site of a monastery in Reading, England, found a mummified hand built into the old foundations – surely the monastery's prized hand of St James, hidden before the building was destroyed. As the church's most important asset, relics were prominently placed in the building. The small chapels off the apse which were so common in the twelfth century were built to display reliquaries. Caskets were fashioned in gold, silver, enamel and jewels to house the remnants, often with small glass windows through which the object could be revered. These caskets themselves were fitted with handled carrying cases so that they could be taken on ceremonial processions.

Artists were hired to paint

pictures of the relics, usually surrounded by scenes from the life of the saint. These paintings themselves commonly became objects of veneration in their own right. Martin Luther, for example (before he began to question such practices), hired Lucas Cranach the Elder to paint some of the 9,000 relics in the collection of the local archbishop as a kind of medieval promotional brochure.

By the early sixteenth century the mania for relics had subsided. The confident humanism of the Renaissance dispelled much of the general fear and insecurity of life and death. The Reformation attacked relics as flagrant idolatry; the violent rampages associated with the Reformation destroyed many of the prominent relics, as well as statues and church furnishings.

THE CRUSADES

Some crusaders marched out of genuine trust that it was 'the will of God' to liberate the Holy Land from the Muslims. But there were other factors. The prospect of winning new lands, coupled with the promise of religious merit, had a great appeal.

There were four major crusades. The first in 1097, reasonably well organized and

highly motivated, managed to capture a number of key cities, including Jerusalem. But subsequent crusades foundered for lack of enthusiasm, funds, and above all, strategists. At last the fourth crusade, detoured from its original plan in an effort to pay its transport debts to the city of Venice, attacked the capital of the Eastern Church, Constantinople. Thus one of the more bizarre architectural effects of the crusades was the dispersal of the spoils of Constantinople.

RIGHT *During their occupation of the Holy Land, the crusaders built churches at important sites. The church of St Anne, Jerusalem, is a beautifully preserved example of crusader architecture.*

BELOW *The crusaders took arms to oust the 'infidel' from holy sites.*

The Viking Craftsmen: Stave Churches

Some of the most intriguing churches ever built grace the rugged Norwegian woodlands. Built in the eleventh to thirteenth centuries, these all-wooden buildings are called 'stave churches' because the timbers used in their construction are like the staves of a barrel.

They are among the earliest churches built in Norway. Christianity came to the region through the Vikings' contact with Christians in England and Ireland. The churches built by these returning sailors are clearly inspired by their familiarity with ship-building. Shipwrights techniques were used throughout; a keel beam ran down the centre of the roof; there were trusses, elbow joints and brackets virtually the same as those of a Viking longboat.

Stave churches were constructed on a sub-frame of massive hewn and notched tree trunks, raised off the ground by boulders. Great masts were mortised into these beams to support the stacked roofs. Working with axe, auger, plane and chisel (saws were an expensive rarity), Norse builders fitted the walls into slots in the beams and locked the joints with well-seasoned wooden nails. The close tolerances they achieved are attested by the fact that, after centuries of storms, some of the churches still stand – their joints still tight.

One unusual feature was an outer 'ambulatory' right round the building. This provided a porch where the people could stamp off the snow – and deposit their weapons! It also helped to protect the foundations of the church.

The interior of the church was dim. A few small windows high in the walls were augmented by candles; many of the initial 800 churches must have collapsed in flames. The chancel was built as an annexe and decorated with large hanging tapestries. Some interiors were painted, but the real decorative forte was wood carving. The writhing, interlocking patterns of the carvings combine the mythical beasts of Norse legends with Christian symbols. The predominant theme of the exterior carving is the adventures of the Norse hero Sigurd. Like others in Norse mythology, he is eternally condemned to endure the effects of his mistakes. These pagan narratives may have been a kind of ready-made local 'Old Testament' for the Norwegians – a prefiguring of Jesus.

The Viking trade routes led to a fertile artistic exchange: the style of the carving is very like Celtic work. It is also possible that the small wooden 'stock' churches of Ireland provided inspiration to the builders of stave churches.

Some of the most delightful decoration occurs in the only metal-work in the building – the doorlock. Iron was painstakingly gathered from the bottom of bogs where sediment from decaying upstream deposits had settled. It was smelted in a highly romantic and difficult procedure and shaped with hammer, tongs and anvil to a finish which would impress the most demanding smith.

Viking converts to Christianity merged some of their old beliefs into their new faith. The dragon-heads on the shingle roofs of stave churches are ancient Viking symbols. This church is at Vik in Norway.

THE ART OF THE CARPENTER

Wood has always been an attractive building material. In some climates well-chosen timber can last almost indefinitely. The stave churches of Scandinavia are a delightful example of both the solidity and warmth of totally wooden structures.

Stone buildings require the use of wood as well, and the carpenter was an essential member of the master builder's army. In the medieval period the master builder himself was expected to be a proficient woodworker.

Timber was usually felled while the foundations for the church were under construction. The trees were chocked up off the ground and left to lie for six months or a year. This seasoning made the timber more stable when cut, and also lightened the load to be transported.

The two most favoured woods were oak and pine, the former for structural work and the latter for scaffolding, centering forms for arches and ceilings, windlasses and general purposes. At the building site timber would be cleft or sawn to rough shape and then prepared with adze and planes. Drawings were made on the shop floor and the carpenter worked with ruler and dividers to transfer these measurements to his work.

Almost all the work was done prior to installing the piece in place. Large beams were awkward to manoeuvre, so there was no point in 'trial and error' fitting. Completed components were numbered and stored until they were needed. For a major construction such as the internal bracing for a tower or steeple, this meant that the carpenter had to have a grasp of the whole construction as well as the parts. During construction pieces would be hoisted up in order and secured with wooden 'tree nails' or trunnels. The holes for these pegs were precisely misaligned so that as the peg was driven in it would pull the joint tight.

The carpenter was also required to make the ladders and scaffolding for the masons. Some of these were ingeniously designed modules which could be easily dismantled and reassembled. During construction of the walls the masons left square holes in the stone work at regular intervals. The scaffolding fitted into these and was held fast by means of wedges.

When the walls were in place, the carpenter could begin assembly of his most important contribution – the roof. The construction of a roof was planned to ensure that the outward thrust against the

BELOW LEFT Tree trunks would be roughly cut to shape where the tree had been felled. RIGHT The finished article, such as this bench end, would not be carved until the wood was fully seasoned.

supporting walls was kept to a minimum. This meant that the roof had to be extensively cross-braced. Each brace had to be fitted to its respective rafters and tie beams. Today these units would be assembled on the ground and then hoisted into position by means of a crane. For the medieval builder it had to be done piece by piece. Obviously the joints had to be made with great precision or the roof would not fit together. It was exhausting and dangerous work.

When the basic structure was complete and the building was watertight the carpenter could begin on the furnishings. There were doors to be made and hung, choir screens to be designed, carved and fitted, and a variety of smaller woodworking tasks. Here the carpenter had the opportunity to show his skills in carving and joinery. Oak was the preferred timber. A large choir screen or reredos (the backing screen over an altar) would again be made in hundreds of pieces and pegged together. The carpenter knew how to position the grain to facilitate carving and cutting mouldings, yet maintain strength. As most churches were unheated the wood tended not to warp or split (until heating was installed in modern times!).

The delicacy of some of this work draws admiration from even the most skilled woodworkers today. The work is infused with a spirit of dedication and good humour. The carpenter may or may not have seen his work as a service to the glory of God, but he clearly felt that only the best was good enough. There is little sign that he used inferior short cuts. In our machine age tools have brought speed and accuracy to woodworking, but these techniques have also bred a dependence on the machines. As a result many of the traditional skills of the carpenter are now near extinction.

Wood was vital both for structural work, such as roof vaults, and for the furnishing of the church, such as the choir screen.

An elaborate choir screen (BELOW) is made from hundreds of parts pegged together. This beautiful pulpit, in contrast, is carved from a single tree trunk!

In New Zealand, wood was plentiful when the cathedral in Auckland was first built; the structure could also resist earthquakes.

The Power and the Glory: Gothic

Grandeur and majesty are the key notes of the church of St Denis in Paris (OPPOSITE). The influential patron wanted the building to express the majesty of God. The result set the style for the whole Gothic style of building.
The 150-foot-high nave of Europe's largest cathedral at Cologne (RIGHT) and the filigree spire of Freiburg cathedral express this same emphasis, pointing upwards to God.

No programme of building in history expresses the conviction and common faith of a people as does the building of churches during the Gothic era. The statistics are astounding. During the twelfth and thirteenth centuries more stone was quarried in France than had been used in ancient Egypt. Foundations for church buildings dropped thirty feet, often with a mass as great as the building above. Spires soared to the height of a forty-storey skyscraper (Strasbourg cathedral) – often the result of plain competitiveness between builders. Amiens cathedral was so vast that the entire population of the city (10,000) could attend at once. Beauvais was built so tall that a fourteen-storey block of flats could fit inside. Winchester cathedral is 556 feet long – enough to fit one and a half football pitches in it.

In France from 1050 to 1350 over 500 large churches were built and tens of thousands of parish churches covered the countryside. There was a church or chapel for every 200 people, a ratio which has never been surpassed. The importance of the church in every sphere of human activity was paramount.

The cause for this dynamic period of building inventiveness cannot easily be isolated. The spread of monastic orders and their organizing influence certainly helped, as did the growth of the pilgrimage routes. By the early eleventh century cities were growing fast, and as the development of civilization is always allied with urban life, it is possible that the intellectual life of the cities spawned the new style.

But if causes are unclear, timing certainly is not. There are few watersheds in architectural history which can be pinpointed as accurately as the Gothic. The style originated in the east end of the Parisian church of St Denis. It was here that a powerful and ambitious church leader by the name of Abbot Suger sought to remodel his church in keeping with the religious thought of the day. A fifth-century Greek theologian called Dionysius was one of the prime contributors to twelfth-century thinking. (At the time he was confused with

Rich materials and textures inside medieval churches added to the majesty of the buildings. This silver chalice comes from Sweden.

a third-century Dionysius, the patron of Paris, and also with a Dionysius who was a contemporary of Paul!) His writings emphasized mystical enlightenment and stressed that the church should be patterned on the heirarchy (he perceived) in heaven. Numerology, the symbolic interpretation of numbers, figured prominently in his work and had already been influential in Byzantine worship. Other Greek philosophers were also read avidly, and their concepts of the 'divine proportions of the universe' seemed to have obvious implications for the building of churches.

Suger and his contemporaries sought to apply this mixture of Greek and Christian thinking to the requirements of the church. Suger also courted the patronage of the royalty and guided the king in the role of the 'apostle of France'. (Secular rulers commonly claimed divine authority, some even termed themselves 'vicars of Christ'.)

The buildings display a more sophisticated knowledge of structural dynamics than is evident in Romanesque work. In particular, the new pointed arches work 'differently' from the old rounded ones. But this feature in itself is not what

makes the new style.

What is different is something less tangible – a sense of order, of lightness in materials and lightness in illumination. Suger and his mastercraftsmen seemed to make the new choir in St Denis (St Dionysius) defy gravity. Gone are the ponderous piers and massive internal buttressing. The walls are thin, the windows large. The ambulatory and radiating chapels are not just mortared together but flow in a harmonious rhythm of pointed arches and slender shafts. All the components have been considered together. Suger was a keen collector and believed that the beauty of God could only be understood through the effect of beautiful things on the senses – quite a radical idea in the Middle Ages!

The effect on kings, peasants and churchmen must have been stunning. Here was a building which transported the visitor in a kind of mystical levitation. It was rational, elegant and mysterious, full of light and opulently decorated.

Suger's builders achieved this effect by some subtle means. The buttresses on the outside of the choir are carefully positioned to be as invisible as possible from inside.

A unique drawing of the west front of Strasbourg cathedral shows something of the craftsmanship that went into every part of the great Gothic churches. A comparison of the plan with the result (RIGHT) shows very few differences.

Pointed arches permit flexibility in the placing of the piers. By carefully positioning supports to receive stress, the architect could use tall thin piers in the place of the ponderous columns of the Romanesque. The result is a space with the three features which were to become the hallmarks of the Gothic style; verticality, achieved through height and visual stress on vertical lines; lightness, created by large windows and slender buttressing; and unity, with all the architectural details integrated into one whole.

The Gothic style quickly spread through western Europe. Itinerant architects carried it to England, Germany, Italy and Spain. There is even a 'French' Gothic cathedral in Upsalla, Sweden. The style changed in

Twin spires are common. The church at Deventer in Holland (ABOVE LEFT) and the great Gothic cathedral at Uppsala in Sweden both have simple and striking spires.

Even small village churches had grand towers. English churches (BELOW) are often decorated with crenellated tops.

contact with local traditions and taste. Where the French had sought great height in the nave, the English produced naves of monumental length. The Italians preferred extensive use of arcading on the exterior, and the Germans became masters of the tower and spire. Though 'high gothic' was primarily a French invention, the many regional interpretations co-mingled. And all shared the same symbolic interpretation.

The burst of building in the twelfth and thirteenth centuries has left lasting monuments not only to the ingenuity and sensitivity of those charged with construction, but also to the elaborate attention given to the clergy. The layman could not participate in the services. It was thought that God was too holy to be approached by untrained people. So the people merely watched the rituals conducted on their behalf.

Because of their education and the authority of church offices, the clergy became a powerful class. Though their role was to be servants of God, the all-too-human temptations of power caused problems. By the late Middle Ages the elite position of the clergy was becoming excessive – and so, too, was their wealth. One particular excess was the sale of spiritual privileges'. Wealthy families would pay large sums to have mass said for them and their deceased relatives in chapels within the church. Charges were also levied for the viewing of relics, for blessings and for special masses. The proliferation of ritual and magic did neither the clergy nor the layman much good. When the authority of the Pope at the top of the pyramid was questioned, tremors were felt right down to the local parish. The great age of Gothic building was only possible because of a total belief in the security and authority of the church. The church in Gothic times was relatively more powerful and influential than government is in our age. There was no shortage of wealthy patrons to finance church building – and there was a considerable degree of competition which also fired the efforts of builders and patrons.

Attempts to revive the Gothic style in the nineteenth century produced many buildings with a superficial resemblance to the great Gothic cathedrals. But the similarity was only superficial. The understanding of the church, of the world, of God's requirements of men had changed in the intervening centuries.

The term 'gothic' was first used in the seventeenth century. Goth-ic meant 'like the uncultured Goths'. It was not meant to be complimentary. 'The external appearance of an old cathedral cannot but be displeasing to the eye of every man who has any idea of propriety and proportion,' says Tobias Smollett in 'Humphry Clinker' (1770). 'Natural imbecility,' complained Sir Henry Wotton in his 'Elements of Architecture'. 'It ought to be exiled from judicious eyes.' Another critic termed Gothic architecture a 'congestion of dark, monkish piles without any just proportion, use or beauty'. Needless to say that negative verdict has been reversed today.

CHARTRES CATHEDRAL

The cathedral of Chartres has been extravagantly praised as the most splendid architectural space in the world. Anyone who has spent a sunny day in its garden of coloured glass and soaring stone stems would probably agree.

In the twelfth century Chartres was a respected intellectual centre, with a monastery, universities, libraries and churches. It had connections with royalty and was essentially a twin capital with Paris. Churches had occupied the town's hilltop site since the eighth century. Though Chartres was not directly on the pilgrimage route, it was itself an object of pilgrimage. The church possessed a highly venerated relic, the tunic of the Virgin Mary. Worship of Mary, rare in the early church, had become very popular by the twelfth century (almost all the major French Gothic cathedrals are dedicated to her) and Chartres considered itself specially favoured in being protected by the Virgin.

In 1194 the old cathedral burnt down. All that remained were the western towers. While the building was still in flames the dean of the cathedral found an architect to undertake the rebuilding. Work started the same year. The dean and the other church officials volunteered three years of their own substantial salaries (the dean's salary alone would have been equivalent to £250,000/$450,000 a year!). Further financing was assured when the Virgin's tunic was discovered unharmed in the rubble-filled crypt. The enthusiasm of the building project is virtually impossible for us to understand: our civilization has no comparable 'centre'. Townsfolk from far and wide brought building materials and provisions. A semi-permanent town-within-a-town was erected to cater for the builders.

Everyone agreed that the new structure was to be far more glorious than the old. Indeed many believed that the Virgin had willed the fire, in order to clear space for a more impressive edifice. But the architectural problems were immense. The existing Romanesque foundations were strong, but the walls were very far apart for a roof as high as the one proposed. The solution was daring. The upper reaches of the nave walls were pierced and lightened by huge windows, and the outward thrust of the roof was supported by a system recently developed in Paris – the flying buttress. The result was in interior space larger, lighter and brighter than any other of the time.

Inside, the architect simplified the nave by eliminating the tribune gallery, which traditionally had been used as a kind of balcony for worshippers. There was liturgical reason for this departure. As the celebration of the Mass had become increasingly important, so a great emphasis had been placed on the viewing of the bread and wine – the 'elements'. Many contemporary accounts tell of worshippers having visions of Christ at the instant when the bread and wine were held aloft. It must be remembered that these were thought to be the actual presence of Christ himself. Doing away with the gallery meant that the whole congregation was united in the nave at this key moment in the service. The simpler nave design also created a greater sense of spatial unity in the sanctuary. This solution was subsequently copied in all the classic cathedrals of France.

The riches of Chartres' decoration are virtually inexhaustible. There are more than 10,000 figures in the

With its weathered copper roof and twin spires, the north one built three hundred years after the simpler south one, the cathedral dominates the town.

Serene figures of kings guard the Royal Portal – the great west door.

sculpture and stained glass. Some scholars have spent more than fifteen years studying the themes in the building! The pictures and story cycles are not merely ornamentation: they are a recitation of the basics of Christian belief applied to every area of life. In an age when few people could read, the building itself told stories. The decoration was an attempt to embody all man's knowledge of the world, and to tell the story of God's action in history. There was a sense that any further learning could only be a refinement of what was already known.

The visible church building was both a symbol and a model for the invisible or 'spiritual' church. The cruciform shape of the church represents both the cross, with the altar as 'head', and the four points of the compass, signifying the extended community of all believers. The church was considered to be a tangible expression of a host of images and ideas expressed in the Bible. It was the body of Christ, a city of refuge, the New Jerusalem, God's presence among men. Some people carried this symbolism to every detail of the building and saw the roof tiles as soldiers of Christ and the steps to the altar as the apostles.

Most of this complex allegory would have been lost on the layman. Indeed even with binoculars it is difficult to make out the figures in the clerestory windows. No matter. Just as the learned theologians could always understand more, so too the cathedral embodied more analogy, allegory and moral symbolism than could ever be grapsed by one person. The very richness of its composition was a symbol for the wealth of God's grace.

The tall columns of the nave reach up elegantly. On the left is the triorium of the south transept.

THE ART OF STAINED GLASS

Glass is as old as the Egyptians, though the glazed window was not developed until Roman times. Cast glass has been found built into the walls of the ruined cities of Pompeii and Herculaneum. Glazed windows were particularly valued in the colder northern climates, but curiously until the tenth century most European glass was imported from Greece. The art of stained glass manufacture began in earnest in the twelfth century.

Coloured glass was produced by adding various metallic oxides (gold, copper, cobalt, manganese and so on) to a molten mixture of sand and potash. (The red produced by this process was of such intensity that it had to be laminated to clear glass so as not to be too dark.) When the right consistency had been achieved, the glass was blown into a cylinder, and unfolded to make a 'sheet'.

The construction of a thirty or forty-foot window was a time consuming craft. This was

French artist Gabriel Loire puts the final leading into a window which shows the story of Noah.

especially true of the early twelfth century windows, when the average size of the fragments was less than two square inches! First the glazier would whitewash a long bench. On this was drawn the placement of the iron bars to support the window. (The joints between lead and glass are very fragile and a large window would collapse from its own weight if it were not wired to this support.)

The design would then be drawn and glass cut to fit. Glass was cut by slowly drawing the tip of a hot iron over the glass – a method which produces a high percentage of rejects. Doubtless these scraps were incorporated into other designs.

When all the glass was cut for a particular part of a design the glazier would then paint the glass with a mixture of iron oxide and a low-melt glaze. The purpose of the painting was not only to treat details too small for glass and lead, but also to control the flow of light through each part of the window. When we look at a bright light in a dark place, we see around it a kind of 'halo' which makes it seem a good deal larger than it really is. So in a stained-glass window the light from each piece of glass tends to 'etch' into the opaque line of the lead strip around it. The glazier often painted the edge of the glass darker where it met the lead to soften the

contrast so that the brightness of each fragment could be controlled. This is an astonishing feat. The unfired glaze looks nothing like it will after the glass has been refired in order to fuse the 'paint' to the surface. The glazier could never really know what a window would look like until it was finished and installed. Working with a small team he proceeded from figure to figure, drawing and copying, squinting and imagining.

The stained glass of the twelfth and thirteenth centuries has rarely been equalled in quality and beauty. The crude manufacturing process produced glass with imperfections which greatly enhance the quality of light. These early windows have a mosaic-like evenness and the jewel-like fragments splinter the light into a rich texture. Later glass, though technically 'better', is often artistically worse, for two reasons. First, improved fabrication produced glass which was uniform in quality – and quite characterless. Second, artists tried to copy the fast-growing techniques of painting. They spent lifetimes trying to reproduce in stained glass effects which can really work only on canvas. The results are rarely as pleasing as the simple mosaics of earlier windows.

If the style of medieval windows was simple, the content was certainly not. They often show complex allegories. A common variety is the 'type–antitype' where an image on the left side of the window is 'explained' by another on the right. The 'Good Samaritan' window from the cathedral of Sens in France is a good example. (It is also interesting because two identical windows were made. The second was originally at Canterbury. There was a fruitful exchange of ideas between English and French glaziers in the twelfth and thirteenth centuries.) The man 'going down from Jerusalem' is compared to Adam leaving

Architects today make use of stained glass to create a particular mood. This is the lantern of the Catholic cathedral in Liverpool, England.

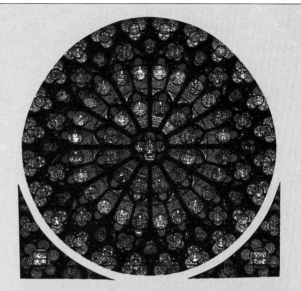

Paradise. He is fallen upon by thieves (the seven deadly sins). The priest and the Levite (the Old Testament Law) pass by and at last the poor man is cared for by the good Samaritan (Christ).

Such riddles were very common. One can almost imagine an earnest prelate explaining the significance of a metaphor to the bemused glazier, tongs in hand. Saints were also popular subject-matter. In the reknowned 'tradesmen's windows' at Chartres each of the windows donated by a guild advertises both their craft and their patron saint.

In the late thirteenth century another type of window was developed, the 'grissaille'. This was predominantly white glass cut in small diamond-shaped panes and decorated with small sections of colour. This had the advantage of letting more light into the church. Indeed a nave illuminated by old glass could be so dark as to make reading impossible on a dull day.

Stained glass windows have

The great south rose window of Notre Dame in Paris, 42 feet/14 metres across, is a collection of Bible stories in glass.

had their enemies. After the Reformation thousands were shattered. In the eighteenth century the English architect Wyatt removed the old glass from Salisbury cathedral to make the nave lighter. He sold the lead for scrap and used the glass to make drainage for the cathedral precincts! Nineteenth-century 'restorers' often made copies of the old windows which to our eyes look characteristically 'nineteenth-century'. Bombs during the two World Wars blew many fine old windows apart. Today the greatest enemy is probably pollution; the old glass is gradually wearing away, eaten by the acidity of the air.

The Church Builders

The great churches and cathedrals were built by professionals. The architect or master mason was familiar with all the various skills which went into the construction of a building. He asked a substantial fee, and got it. Travelling with a team of trusted workers he supervised every aspect of the work. Groups of masons even organized conferences to discuss building techniques – attracting masons from many countries. Each mason had his own drawings and cloth rolls containing essential measurements, angles, and means of calculating stress, which were his reference book. He often actually owned quarries.

After drawings were accepted by the patron, the first task was to organize delivery of materials. Anyone building in the twentieth century knows how difficult and aggravating this job can be; it used to be worse. Until the nineteenth century it was common to transport building materials by ox-cart and barge; the former meant that roads had to be built and the latter not uncommonly meant diverting rivers! River transport was preferred because of cost and load capacity. Stone would sometimes be finish-cut in the quarry and given a mark to indicate its final position in the building. Another mark would show who had cut it, since the workers were paid per block.

Supplies were often given to building projects, but this generosity could be subject to abuse. One benefactor gave a bishop permission to cut 'as much timber as his men could remove in four days and nights'. Imagine his fury when the bishop brought 'an innumerable troop' and denuded a large part of his forest!

Facilities set up on site would include a host of stone-cutters' workshops, kilns for burning lime to make mortar, saw pits for cutting timber, forges for making metalwork, other kilns for glaziers and store houses for materials and tools. The basic tools of the stone-cutter were mallets, bow drills and chisels. Perhaps the most interesting tools were those used for measuring and 'machines' for lifting heavy weights. Measuring tools were simple, but in expert hands could produce work to extremely fine tolerances. To find a right angle for reference the builder would lay out a triangle with sides three, four and five units long; the two shorter sides joined at 90°. The architect could check the accuracy of the strings stretched out for foundations, and other angles could be derived from the right angle. Two sets of footing walls were built, one to carry the arcades and the other to support the exterior buttresses.

After the foundations had set and settled (a year or two) the first courses of stone would be laid at the east end of the building. Mirrors and water-filled wooden troughs were used to check horizontal levels, and plumb-lines to check the verticals. Working from east to west the builders would first raise the internal arcade and then the walls and buttressing. To lift the cut stones into place a variety of windlasses were used, often large man-powered 'squirrel cages' with a rope wound round one shaft. Smaller loads of stone and mortar were carried with hods or wooden buckets. Scaffolding was usually erected by leaving holes in the walls where horizontal beams could be inserted and roped to vertical supports.

The construction of vaults required experience. First the shape of the ribs would be drawn on a 'tracing floor' – a large white-washed or plaster-covered floor. Templates were made from these drawings so that the cutting of the stone could be checked continually. A wooden centering form was then built to the inside dimensions of the arch and this was secured to a movable scaffolding under the first bay to be vaulted. The stones were laid along the centering from alternate sides until at last the keystone was put in place. When both ribs were in place the centering would be moved to the next bay and so on down the nave. Additional forms were used to support the infill between the ribs – though in some churches this is only rubble, straw and plaster.

The main difficulty in the construction of church towers was the problem of height. Scaffolding had to be constructed on site, so that heavy components could be brought up in stages. But the difficulties did not deter the craftsmen from showing real care.

Few large churches or cathedrals were built in a generation. Most were constructed over centuries, with later styles superimposed on the earlier. In some places, such as the transept of Winchester

Lifting materials into place was one of the difficulties the builders face. Elaborate machinery was designed to do the job.

Cathedral, evidence of the improvement in construction technique during the period of building can be seen; the later joints are thinner and the surfaces more precisely worked. Standards for measurement might also change. At one time in England the basic unit was the rod, which was determined by marking out the length of sixteen grown men's feet! A later mason might very well arrive with another standard – for there was no efficient co-ordination of measurement until well into the seventeenth century.

Because of the time such a building required to construct, it was generally put to use for services well before completion. A temporary wooden 'west end' closed the building off, and oil-soaked linen filled the window spaces. The sound of chisels, the creak of wooden gears and the shuffle of feet on boards high overhead must have made a curious accompaniment to the chanting of the mass. One can understand the great ceremonies which attended the consecration of each completed section of the building.

THE ART OF THE BUILDERS AND MASONS

Many do-it-yourself enthusiasts have worked with wood at some time or other, but few have attempted to cut stone. The specialist stone-cutters today rely on tools such as diamond-edged power-saws, pneumatic chisels and high-speed engraving tools, and use protective goggles. To cut flowing organic forms from stone with a mallet and chisels thus seems even more of a feat.

Just as it is easier to carve lime wood than ash, so too each type of stone has its own 'grain' and other characteristics. Certain types of stone have always been pre-ferred for carving ornate capitals; others are better for constructing walls. The master builder therefore had to have a good eye for stone. He had to evaluate the qualities of local stone, and work out the quantities required.

The first job at the quarry was to free large chunks of rock so that it could be cut into the required shapes. This was done in several ways. Holes were drilled into the stone during the winter and filled with water. When the water froze it would expand, splitting the rock. Another method was to light fires which would heat the rock and then to cool the rock suddenly by pouring water on it to make it split.

Once the boulders had been freed the masons could go to work. The master builder would supply the dimensions, and each mason would have his own ruler, square, and calipers. Lines would be drawn on the surface with chalk. Chisels with coarsely serrated edges were used to rough out the work. Final shaping and polishing were sometimes accomplished by rubbing the stones on another hard flat stone. Most of the basic build-ing stones would be cut and shaped in the quarry and given the mark of the workman (workmen were generally paid per stone). These dressed stones are called ashlar.

Pieces destined to become capitals or moulded sections were usually transported to the mason's lodge at the building site. Here there was a drawing floor covered with chalk or plaster. Using a combination of flat drawings and wooden templates, the master carver made the more complex com-ponents. Important carvings such as capitals and statues were roughed out in the lodge and then installed before finishing. This eliminated the risk of damaging fragile under-cuttings during installation.

Stone carving is very laborious, and bits which break off cannot easily be 'glued' on. The master carver needed to be a patient sort, but efficient and fast. In addition he needed to be sensitive to the wishes of the patron and aware of the latest stylistic developments. The secrets of the craft were carefully guarded among the masons.

The next time you look at stone carving try to imagine what it would be like to carve some of those intricate shapes. Imagine the steady tapping of

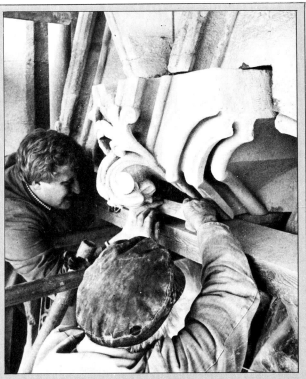

the mallet, the flying chips of stone, the dust and the constant measuring. Try to envisage the atmosphere of the workshop, the stories, the comments made by other stone cutters, the long hours and the cold feet. It was hard work, a labour which placed an emphasis on time and accomplishment which it is difficult for us to understand today.

A piece of stone is precisely cut to size and carved.

The Ascent of Man: the Renaissance

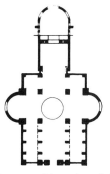

Renaissance architects drew their inspiration from classical forms. Church plans were far more compact than Gothic ones.

Commissioned by Pope Julius II in the early 1500s, the monumental new St Peter's in Rome (OPPOSITE) was worked on by all the famous architects of the time. The result was a triumphal statement of the institutional church's power and the builders' genius.

BELOW *The sculpted gold doors of the great Florence baptistry. Portrayals of biblical scenes were now not 'other worldly' but lifelike.*

The Italian architect Alberti was a prototype of what was to become in the late Renaissance the ideal man. He built churches and public buildings; he was an accomplished horesman and athlete; he studied law, physics and mathematics; he painted, wrote plays, poems, music and a treatise on economy, and was renowned for his dazzling wit.

Alberti and the other great architects of the Renaissance – Bramante, Raphael and Michelangelo – enjoyed a new type of artistic prestige. Rather than being skilled tradesmen building churches for the needs of the Christian community, they were artists, expressing their insights. Fifteenth-century Italy was quite prepared to acknowledge earthly as well as heavenly brilliance. Even before the Renaissance the architect had been highly regarded, but now the artist's vision was regarded as sacred. And over the centuries, this shift from tradesman to visionary has had a profound affect on the role of the artist.

A dramatic change in ideas about man in the fifteenth and early sixteenth century brought about a revision of cultural, political, economic and church life. The new thinking began in Florence, spread throughout Italy and then followed the trade routes north.

Already in the late Gothic period the combination of Greek thought with Christian concepts had gradually focussed thinking men's attention on the nature of man himself. Art of the time shows this. Portrayals of Christ began to stress his human nature, for example; representation of saints were less concerned with symbolism and more with anatomy. In all walks of life, the nobility of man was becoming the key theme. In Italy this humanism grew with the development of a merchant class. Independent traders and bankers seemed to fare quite well without an unduly subservient attitude to the church. New commentaries on Greek philosophy emphasized the nobility of man and the individual's need to take his potential into his own hands. Artists became more highly regarded, too, and found a new source of patronage in the merchants to supplement their reliance on the church.

The church, of course, was still a powerful institution. Indeed, the Renaissance popes readily adopted the manners and pretensions of secular rulers. In the cultivated self-awareness of the age, they sought to modernize the church in keeping with their own confidence.

Church building was often sponsored by princes and merchants as well as the clergy, so the requirements of services were not usually the main concern. This can be seen simply by looking at the ground plans of most Renaissance churches. The chancel is smaller, the crossing larger. The dome over the crossing has become the true focus of the church. The scale of the buildings has also changed radically. The soaring height of a Gothic nave made a person feel dwarfed, humble and contrite. Now the Renaissance churches are scaled to a more 'human' level.

The vertical stress of the High Gothic has been replaced by a careful balance of proportions. The mystical space of a Gothic church is gone, and the tangible mass of walls and sculpture have once more been emphasized. For example, the standard arrangement of side aisles is altered by making each bay a separate chapel, slowing down the speed at which the eye can 'take in' the building.

In the Middle Ages it was generally acknowledged that construction of a church took more than a lifetime. Like an ancient tree, a cathedral would sprout new branches from generation to generation. But the Renaissance was concerned with wholeness, and so it was unthinkable that a church should be altered after it had been built. When Pope Pius II had a cathedral built in his home town of Pienza he decreed that no one should ever add or remove anything, or even alter the colour scheme of the interior.

The church architecture of the Renaissance is rather like entries in a competition, with each new building trying to be more perfectly proportioned and detailed than the last. New methods of construction were developed, and there was an excited dialogue among the architects and intellectuals. But the life of the church does not always move at the same pace as the building. The same ideas which produced Renaissance churches eroded the faith that the buildings were supposed to serve.

Back to Basics: the Reformation

By the late fifteenth century the church knew it was in trouble. Laxity and corruption was wide-spread amongst the clergy and authorities seemed deaf to the pleading for a crackdown to save the church. Rome dragged its feet. Running the ecclesiastical bureaucracy was costly and reforms would certainly reduce revenue.

While the church dithered Europe exploded. Movements of protest and reform had already prepared people for the inevitable revolt against a corrupt and oppressive system. Renaissance learning and a new class of literate activists questioned both the doctrine and policy of the church. The development of cheap printing encouraged people to read, compare and draw their own conclusions. By 1500 over 30,000 titles were in circulation in Europe – most of them religious works. So when Martin Luther in Germany publicly protested against the practice of 'selling tickets to heaven' to raise money for St Peter's Church in Rome, there were plenty of others to support him. The issue of course went deeper. Can we earn our way to heaven by good works, or is it, as Luther discovered for himself in the New Testament, a matter of trusting in God's grace alone?

Luther in Germany, Calvin in Geneva, Zwingli in Zurich thrashed out the theology of the issues. The response from the church authorities was defensive. Popular support was enormous: the new message was a liberating one.

But one response to the teaching of Luther and the other reformers' was a wave of idol-smashing iconoclasm. The reformers rejected many traditional church practices: confession, pilgrimage, relics, prayers for the dead, clerical celibacy and ecclesiastical wealth. These had no foundation in the Bible and undermined the gospel of faith in Jesus Christ as being all that is necessary to approach God. Rowdy crowds tore down monasteries, smashed statues and stained glass – and displayed none of the virtues of spiritual enlightenment. The reformers tried to restrain them, but the church was an easy target, rich and soft.

'Protestantism', as it was to be called, took hold. By the mid-sixteenth century Western Europe was firmly divided between Catholics and Protestants. The Catholic church did eventually institute far-reaching reforms, but the breach was too wide to be closed.

It was one thing to throw bricks through stained-glass windows and quite another to develop alternatives to the medieval pattern of worship. The kernel of Reformation thought was that people could not enter into a relationship with God, or grow in that relationship, without hearing the gospel preached. The focus of worship shifted from the ritual re-enactment of Christ's death at the altar to the preaching of God's word from the pulpit. The cavernous old churches, well suited to creating a sense of mystery, were acoustically dreadful for preaching. This became even worse after the removal of the rejected choir-screens, icons and altars which symbolized the separation of priest from people.

How could the building, then, be made to suit the people's needs? The reformers did not eliminate the communion table, but gave it a position of less prominence. The pulpit was moved into the nave, generally attached to one of the pillars. A large sounding-board behind it helped combat echo. The sermon became a fixed part of the service, and so benches were provided for the congregation to sit in a semi-circle beneath the pulpit. Sometimes an additional reading desk or lectern was built on the opposite side of the nave. The whole idea of what the communion service meant

Changes to churches after the Reformation show dramatically how beliefs are expressed in church buildings. Zwingli's church at Zürich, Switzerland is typical of churches throughout Protestant Europe: the altar for the celebration of the mass, high in the chancel was removed; seats were put in its place. The focus was now the pulpit half-way down the nave.

changed. The reformers considered that it was not a re-enactment of Christ's sacrifice, but a celebration of what that sacrifice meant. The people were now to take part in it. In some churches, the table was moved from the position of 'altar' at the east end of the church down to the chancel steps. Simple wooden tables were used instead of stone altars.

Chantry chapels, no longer used to say mass for the deceased, were sometimes converted to libraries or teaching rooms or used for wedding services. The multi-coloured medieval wall paintings were painted out.

The resulting space was cool, bright and large. The seventeeth-century Dutch painter Pieter Saenredam gives us a good idea what Dutch Reformed churches looked like in the 1600s. The nave remained open through the week and was a popular meeting place.

The austerity of the all-white interior was softened by the gradual accumulation of monuments, plaques with creeds and the like. But the biggest introduction was generally the organ.

The early stages of Protestantism did not require new church buildings; the

Protestants took over the existing church buildings and adapted them for their own use. But as old buildings fell into disrepair and as congregations grew, new facilities for worship were required. The new buildings reflected the doctrinal shift from altar to pulpit. There was much experimentation with the shape of the church in an effort to permit the preacher to use a normal speaking voice. 'L' form, 'T' form, cross,

The Pilgrim Fathers were radical Protestants who sought a new start, away from repressive European state churches. This church built in 1686 shows how their building style reflected their 'clean sweep' attitude.

St Andrew's, Holborn Circus (LEFT) *was one of the churches Sir Christopher Wren built in London after the Great Fire of 1666. With its gallery, dominant organ and pulpit and classical style it is an elegant expression of formalized post-Reformation protestantism.*

BELOW *The artist Pieter Saenredam recorded what Dutch churches looked like in the seventeenth century when they had been cleared out after the Reformation.*

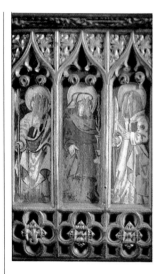

The Reformation had its destructive side. All over Europe, beautiful carvings were defaced and stained glass smashed as people revolted against medieval abuses.

A meeting of Quakers (RIGHT) typifies the radical Reformation groups. Most, such as the Anabaptists, stressed the sole authority of the Bible without the need for church hierarchies. They were the forerunners of Baptist churches today. Congregational and other churches also date from these 'gathered churches' which stressed the 'priesthood of all believers'.

round, oval, polygon – virtually everything was tried. They all attempted to concentrate on the principle liturgical centres of pulpit, communion table and font.

Later, a major innovation was the introduction of the gallery, which made it possible to fit a larger congregation into a smaller space. The English architect, Wren, even conducted experiments to determine the maximum permissible distance from the pulpit in all directions before 'clarity' was lost. Hearing the preacher became the main consideration in church design. With the advent of galleries, pulpits grew taller to reach up to them. In the Frauenkirche in Dresden (1738) there were five tiered galleries and the pulpit was at the second-storey level! Many free church buildings still used today are built with galleries, no chancel, but impressive positions for preacher and organ.

In the New World, architects had a clean slate. America in the seventeenth and eighteenth centuries was full of architectural experiment. Traditional English church styles were reinterpreted in the most abundant local material – wood. The Anglicans (Episcopalians) tended to build rather nostalgic imitations of medieval English parish churches, complete

with carved chancel screens. Puritan building, on the other hand, tried half-a-dozen different liturgical arrangements, all of which stressed the position of the pulpit. The form of the parish church devised by Wren and Gibbs became rooted in America in the nineteenth century, and produced some of the most attractive 'post colonial' buildings.

The Reformation could not instantaneously produce its own architecture. By trial and error it settled on a variety of 'hall-church' types. Reformed churches tend to emphasize clarity, order and solemnity, features which can produce elegant architecture, but can also be quite plain and boring. The desire to make these church interiors more 'spiritual' was one of the key motivations behind the nineteenth century revival of 'ancient styles'.

LEFT *The reformers realized that through new hymns with popular music, it would be possible to 'sing the Reformation into the hearts of the people.' The organ soon became an important feature in churches.*

The Drama of Religion: Baroque

The style known as Baroque was both new and a continuation of the elaborate sculptural building of the High Renaissance. It received impetus from several sources.

The Protestant Reformation (which coincided with the High Renaissance) presented a frightening challenge to the Roman church. At the Council of Trent in the mid-sixteenth century the Catholic church set about putting its house in order. Reforms in church doctrine and practice were easier now because by the time of the Council virtually all the dissenters had left. The founding of the missionary and teaching order, the Society of Jesus (the Jesuits) was part of the same aim – to reunite the church under the papacy. The restored authority was used to organize the church both administratively and liturgically, and as a result of these efforts the Catholic church regained many areas lost to the Protestants in the Reformation. By the seventeenth century national boundaries, governments and religions were more clearly defined than ever before. Northern Germany, Scandinavia, the Netherlands and England remained predominantly Protestant. France was Catholic but less dependent on the papacy than Italy, Spain and Portugal.

The Baroque style developed most quickly in these southern areas, but was not limited to them. Neither was it purely a Catholic style – though later it was thought to be so. The missionary excursions to Central and South America in the eighteenth century helped fortify the Roman church and the Baroque style soon took root there, blending with the local forms of decoration to produce churches of astonishing complexity.

The early Baroque churches in Italy are characterized by a sense of drama and mystical religious feelings. The cool experiments of the Renaissance yield to the urge for more emotional experience. Catholic theology placed great importance on the mass as a dramatic re-enactment of Christ's death, on savouring the mysteries of the gospel and on feeling the wounds of Christ suffered on one's behalf. As a result, everything about the churches has emotional and symbolic meaning. Through

The church at Wies in Bavaria is a lavish example of the Baroque style. The almost overwhelming ornamentation is designed to exalt the worshipper, emphasising the drama and mystery of religion.

Details such as sculpture (BELOW) and metalwork all contributed to the overall effect.

The Baroque style began in Italy. The church of Sant'Ignazio in Rome (CENTRE) dates from the 1690s. Its extraordinary ceiling was designed to appear like the gate of heaven itself.

The style of European Baroque churches, such as the church of Vierzehnheiligen in South Germany (LEFT) was taken by Jesuit missionaries to other parts of the world, such as Mexico (RIGHT).

the lavish texture of the interior the worshipper is to be caught up into the realm of the infinite. Led by the senses, he is intended to transcend them.

In essence Baroque church architecture returns to the medieval spirit. But the means used are quite different. The medieval cathedral focussed on the sacramental elements; the Baroque church was an all-encompassing totality. The skills of orchestrating sensual experience, refined in the Renaissance, were put to full use in the Baroque.

The church buildings were metaphors for the gates of heaven itself. In many churches this is almost literally true. The ceiling is a painted illusion of the heavens; the whole roof of the building dissolves into the glorious realms above. Theatrical means are employed throughout the building, and these relate to the events taking place over the altar – the ascension of the Virgin, St Michael and the Dragon or the vision of a saint. These churches work like cinema: they have plot, sustained drama and conclusion. Ingeniously placed windows spotlight the dramatic groups.

Compared to the writhing interiors, Baroque exteriors are relatively plain.

Straight lines are often modulated with curves and the sheer bulk of the church is emphasized. The Baroque churches of South America are an exception in that they are rarely plain, and when there is abundant ornament it is richly coloured.

The magnificent church of Vierzehnheiligen ('The Fourteen Saints') in Northern Bavaria, Germany, is a good example of late Baroque at its most sophisticated. The west front is calm and stately. The interior is so complex that it is impossible to 'understand' it without referring to a ground plan. In fact the nave is comprised of four interlocking ovals, with circular transept arms. The oval plan became popular in the second half of the seventeenth century and seems to epitomize the builders' urge to make the church a symbol of the union of heaven and earth.

The refinement of the Baroque style, lighter and less frenzied, is known as Rococo. Rococo ornamentation is more abstract and 'frothy' than the Baroque, and less obviously theatrical. By the late eighteenth century several other stylistic currents were blending with the Baroque and Rococo. In particular, the world of ancient Greece and Rome was once again a key influence.

The Baroque church is an exuberant chorus of sensory experience designed to foster spiritual vision. This direct effect on the senses has proved to have a continuing appeal; indeed there are few Baroque churches which are not still in use today, and Baroque forms of decoration still sell well in our machine age.

Every part of the building was richly decorated. This door is from a church in Spain.

THE EXPORTED CHURCH

People take their beliefs with them when they travel. European commerce in the sixteenth and seventeenth centuries opened trade routes to Asia, Africa and the New World.

The most vigorous exporters of the church were the Jesuits who combined trade with missions in South America, India and the Philippines. They supervised church construction and trained locals in building techniques. Invariably their churches have a pronounceed regional style. The elaborate Mexican churches, for instance, owe as much to the local Indian style of convoluted carving as they do to the Spanish Baroque tradition.

Missionaries had a difficult decision: should they 'christianize' the local religious architecture, or should they import Western forms which would be free of misleading associations with the old religions? They usually chose the latter. Today the balance has shifted. New churches often follow local forms.

The cultural cross-currents of the exported church have generated many mixed styles – but also some beautiful buildings.

Many churches in 'mission areas', such as this chapel in Fiji, were built in imitation of traditional European styles. Today there is greater emphasis on reflecting local styles and culture.

In the eighteenth century Central America was an important missionary area.

Missionaries taking their faith to other cultures have realized that there is nothing particularly sacred about their own forms of worship, let alone buildings. This simple meeting place is in East Malaysia.

The Birth of the Modern Age

In the mid-eighteenth century the established church was in decline. Science and philosophy were growing fast, and the idea of Progress captured the minds of the people as religion had done in earlier ages. The brash new philosophers not only attacked the bureaucracy of religion but even dared to question the existence of God.

What began as an intellectual ferment soon became a revolutionary political action. The American Revolution delivered a blow to the old order. Then the Enlightenment, born in the drawing room of aristocratic French idealists, became a revolution which shook the foundations of Europe. The Industrial Revolution, though not overtly religious or political, ensured that the old order would never return. In France, part of the violence was directed against the established church. Many beautiful buildings including St Denis and Cluny were badly damaged, and it was proposed that Chartres should be pulled down and replaced with a 'temple of wisdom'.

Yet curiously this turbulent century was also a period of religious revival. In America, England, the Netherlands and Germany itinerant preachers revitalized churches. The Moravians and Methodists particularly had a strong missionary outlook. Preaching in the open air, tents, houses or wherever they could, they brought a spirit of conviction to their testimony of God's love. Waves of revival swept the Protestant nations.

One result was that scores of churches were built by new groups of Christians. It is hardly surprising that the building was sporadic and stylistically varied. By and large, the Rococo style was rejected as being unsuitably frivolous. The simple functional style was Neo-classic, yet another return to the source of Roman antiquity. Neo-classicism differed from earlier classical revivals in being both more consistent and more austere. New revelations about classical styles came through excavations of the Roman town of Pompeii and caught the imagination of architects and people alike.

By this time the position of the professional architect had been firmly established and architectural practices had been set up. The Roman styles were carefully analyzed and measured drawings of columns, capitals and pediments were

American churches of the eighteenth century (LEFT) *have a simple, graceful style. The layout, with no lower side aisles, is known as a 'hall church', reflecting the hall-type meeting-places of the radical Reformation.*

In England, the aristocracy sometimes built churches in their own estates. This private church shows the influence of Italian architecture.

circulated. Wren's famous church of St Paul's in London marks the transition between the Baroque and the classical. The staggering variety of churches he built after the great London fire of 1666 shows both his own ingenuity and the desire to make churches more rational, orderly and usable. In France the earliest Neo-classical church, Ste Geneviève (1755) was converted into a 'temple of reason' during the French revolution.

The calm, stately orders of Neo-classicism had a great influence on even the most modest of church buildings. Methodist meeting halls were fronted with graceful pilasters and columns, and 'classic' Georgian architecture enhanced many of the new churches of the Atlantic seaboard. Besides the imposing columns, stressed quoins and heavy cornices, Neo-classical designers favoured the central plan, surmounted when possible with a dome. Neo-classicism was to have its greatest effect on civic architecture, as can be seen in virtually any capital in Europe.

Generally Neo-classical styles had the widest distribution in countries most affected by the thinking of the Enlightenment – England, France, Germany and the then young United States. In Scandinavia the change was less pronounced and the traditional local forms persisted. Spain apparently found it difficult to relinquish the love of ornament and the austerity of Neo-classical architecture made few inroads there.

Alongside Neo-classicism, another architectural current was also strong –

St Paul's Cathedral in London is the finest church built by Sir Christopher Wren. It is Baroque in its feeling, but the techniques are neo-Classical.

The exciting revival of faith which was begun by itinerant preachers such as the Wesleys led to the building of many small chapels – often in quiet agricultural communities!

Romanticism. Some architects and artists disliked the emphasis on the cold light of reason and longed for an architecture that was mysterious and (that most important eighteenth-century word) 'sublime'. In particular, the Romantics admired the Gothic cathedrals. Goethe was rapturous about their emotive effect and the German artist Casper David Friedrich made the ruined Gothic cathedral the symbol of his own mystical pantheism. The nineteenth century, popularizing eighteenth-century Romantic theory, was to see in the once-despised 'Gothick' the only 'true Christian architecture'.

The clean lines of neo-classicism are clear in this American church.

Forwards or Backwards? The Nineteenth Century

In 1800 most of western Europe was dominated politically by Napoleon's France and intellectually by the ideals of the Enlightenment. Science, industry and philosophy appeared to be making great strides and there was a romantic optimism about the future of mankind, an optimism which was decidedly secular.

This hope for a bright future coupled with a new interest in the order and beauty of Greek culture gave birth to an architectural style called Romantic Classicism. Arcades of Ionic columns sprang up on public buildings, shopping arcades and church façades. Until this time, Christians had rejected the Greek temple as an architectural model because of its pagan associations. But this was no barrier to the nineteenth-century designers who saw in the temple not paganism but order.

The interest in classical antiquity was

What are the nineteenth-century church builders trying to achieve? St Patrick's cathedral in the heart of New York (RIGHT) harks back to the fourteenth-century rather than relating to the tower blocks which now surround it.

As well as building new churches, architects carefully renovated old buildings. The Dutchman P. J. H. Cuijpers rebuilt this Romanesque church.

matched by an enthusiasm for the Middle Ages. In both France and England there was revived interest in Catholic liturgy. The Anglo-Catholic movement of nineteenth-century England was a conscious effort to recapture the mystery, beauty and intensity of worship. An idealized view of medieval life led to conscious attempts to imitate Romanesque and Gothic buildings. These styles seemed to have an inherent 'spiritual' quality about them, a quality which more and more people were beginning to miss in the new 'machine age'. By mid-century it was becoming apparent that the 'triumph of reason' was making much of the social fabric quite unreasonable. Devout revivalists hoped to provide an alternative by rediscovering the lost essence of religion.

Yet the attempts to infuse church buildings with devotion were not particularly successful. The best-informed architects of the period, such as England's Pugin and France's Viollet le Duc studied ancient building in detail. The majority, unfortunately, simply copied things from books or from other architects. Their productions are uniformly boring. Why? For one thing, there was little sensitivity to the past periods of architecture. Components were selected from each, almost at random. The beginnings of the communication era meant that most architects could be aware of the work of others. Shared information brought with it uniformity. Nineteenth-century churches throughout Europe are quite similar. The prime model for most nineteenth-century architects was the French Gothic cathedral. Countless style-books circulated and similar forms were pasted onto buildings almost at random.

The latest technical advances also brought problems. Constructional short cuts eliminated the need for that logic of design which had determined the form of the great medieval cathedrals. It was possible to make steel pillars to hold the church up and then to box them in with machine-cut stone. The effect somehow is not 'right'.

The biggest problem with the revival of old styles is really a philosophical one. Why do we try to express ourselves with someone else's words, or make suitable places for worship with the style of another age? The uncomfortable answer, of course, is that we do not know what style is appropriate for our own age. The nineteenth century's frenetic pace of life sent traditional values tumbling in a maelstrom of change. There was nothing to fill the void except imports from the past. But the imported style was stranded without its most essential support – the social and religious base on which cathedrals were built. It is for this reason that many nineteenth-century Neo-gothic, Neo-classical, or Neo-romanesque churches were never a happy experiment.

Revivalism continues in the twentieth century. There are still 'Gothic' cathedrals under construction (though very few recent commissions). The cost of completing them is now astronomical. If nothing else, they are a testament to the enduring success of their ancestors: when we think of a glorious church, the Gothic cathedral naturally comes to mind.

Despite its attempt to turn back the clock, the nineteenth century did make its own contributions to the development of church architecture. The restoration of old buildings, though over-zealous, saved many structures from dilapidation and collapse.

As the secular philosophies of the Enlightenment threatened the church, some groups responded by trying to define their doctrine more specifically. Some believed that the church should be organized differently – for example, with a group of 'non-professional' leaders rather than one full-time paid clergyman. Here the Enlightenment's emphasis on freedom had another effect; many Christians felt that if they were unhappy with existing church structures and organizations there was no reason why they should not start another church more to their liking. But these 'non-conformist' churches were not just a reaction against the established state churches. They were also a response to the renewed spiritual life that the new emphasis on evangelism was bringing to the churches.

New religious groupings produced many variations on the galleried hall-church, using iron pillars in place of stone. Some of the churches have great charm as well as a practical layout designed for the needs of the congregation. Invariably these buildings are of greater interest than the many revivalist attempts. The proliferation of small churches and chapels provided for the needs of a growing population. The multiplication of church buildings in the nineteenth century rivalled the building surge of the twelfth century. But the church itself was under attack, and putting up buildings could not shore up a crumbling institution.

Cuijpers' church of St Agatha and St Barbara at Oudenbosch (LEFT) *is a direct copy of St Peter's in Rome.*

In England and France, the nineteenth century was a time of revived interest in medieval life. Architects such as Pugin used modern techniques to recreate the atmosphere of medieval churches. This rich, dark chapel at Cheadle in England (BELOW) *gives a real sense of mystical religion.*

ODDITIES OF CHURCH DESIGN

Escaping from persecution, Christians in Göreme, Turkey, hollowed out volcanic rocks to make tiny churches and monasteries.

Every age has its dissidents, visionaries and nuts. Some start political parties or art movements; some perform feats of endurance or set out to walk around the world backwards; some build churches. They can become cult heroes or outcasts – sometimes both. History periodically reviews their achievements and decides whether they are due for revival or ridicule. The church builders either believe that they are providing for an as yet unrealized need – for example a floating church – or simply do what seems appropriate to them.

Only occasionally are their extreme forms backed by groups of Christians who actually mean to use the building. Most often these maverick buildings are the pet projects of an architect or a determined and wealthy individual. The bizarre schemes often call for unusual materials or techniques.

The Floating Church of the Redeemer for Seamen at Philadelphia was built in New York in 1851. It floated on the twin hulls of two clipper ships; its exterior was painted to resemble brown stone and inside it was complete with groined vault and bishop's throne.

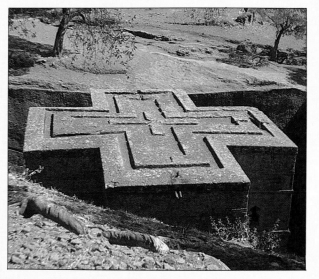

At Lalibela in Ethiopia are some extraordinary seven-hundred-year-old churches built vertically downwards. They are carved out of the solid rock.

Temples or Meeting Places? Church Building Today

A group of Christians meeting today to discuss plans for a new church building has a difficult task. It is awkward enough to agree on delicate matters of budget, but it is virtually impossible to be in accord about 'style'. In a sense, there are too many options.

Regrettably, many contemporary churches seem to have been constructed primarily to look impressive – and indeed they do – rather than to meet the actual requirements of an actual worshipping congregation. Churches have been built in the shape of a fish or a crown of thorns, but these symbolic forms in no way relate to the actual practical use of the space.

Part of the problem stems from a conception of worship which makes going to church like going to the theatre or lecture hall. The word 'auditorium' is often used in reference to churches, and the personality of a preacher is too often the prime element in the service. Passive worship becomes the norm, though in fact passive worship is a contradiction in terms. The most extreme example of this is the American 'television church'. Broadcast services in America are followed by millions of viewers, many of whom would otherwise be unlikely to make the effort physically to attend church. The movements of the television camera and the studio-mixed sound of the organ can undoubtedly communicate, but these services lack the active personal contact which is so crucial to the church as a 'body of believers'.

Yet building practical and attractive churches in the modern style is possible – and preferable to attempts to cling to Gothic imitations. Invariably the modern church building which 'works' is the result of a careful review by the congregation of what the 'church' means and what elements of their life together are important. By consultation with an architect, various methods of achieving those ends can be compared. The technical possibilities of building in our century are greater than ever before. Reinforced concrete components can be made at a factory and bolted together on site. The strength of modern components means that walls no longer have to be massive. Modern building techniques are now similar to furniture making: the strength of the joints is the most critical calculation. With an internal frame of steel or pre-stressed concrete the outside of the building need not be load-bearing. It is possible to make a roof which holds up curtain-like walls of shimmering glass.

But the technical ability and the personal enthusiasm of architects has not guaranteed success. Looked at from the point of view of architecture, one reason why there is no distinctive twentieth-century 'church style' is simply that there is no distinctive twentieth-century architectural style. After the immense shock of the First World War, architects were among the most prominent voices clamouring for change. Many honestly believed that only a renewed and reconstituted environment could establish values and bring about peace. The choice, said the famous French architect Le Corbusier, is 'architecture or revolution'. It has taken us a long time to realize that their visionary utopias of architecture are only possible in a totalitarian state, and that

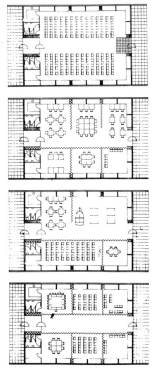

Today church buildings are designed to be used not just for use one day a week. This simple hall in the new city of Milton Keynes in England can be used for worship for 224 people, for children's activities, for film shows, a boat-building club and senior citizen's meetings.

In Asia and South America church-building has a special problem – the phenomenal rate of church growth. This church in Seoul, South Korea (LEFT) is doubling its membership every eighteen months. The main auditorium holds 11,000: six Sunday services are telecast to dozens of other buildings.

Le Corbusier's chapel of Notre Dame du Haut, one of the most famous buildings in this century, was not built for a congregation of Christians at all. It is a pilgrimage church. Inside, it seats only fifty people. The occasional vast group of pilgrims stay outside – a pulpit and altar are built on the outside wall specially for them.

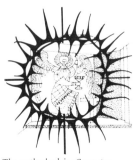

The cathedral in Coventry, England, was destroyed in the Second World War. The new cathedral contains works of art by leading British artists, such as this huge crown of thorns.

A small, simple Baptist church in Stockholm, Sweden.

OPPOSITE, ABOVE *Christmas is celebrated at the Roman Catholic cathedral in Bristol, England. The large, low area for the congregation can be used in a variety of ways.*

*No less than in other periods, today churches are built for many reasons. The Taivallahti church in Helsinki, Finland (*BELOW*) was designed for a competition in 1960. But as well as being an exciting construction, sunk in a rock crater, it is also an imaginatively designed meeting-place.*

living in orderly ranks of tower blocks can be numbing and degrading.

After the Second World War there was a building spree of unprecedented proportions. About three-quarters of the buildings were utilitarian blocks with no pretensions to being 'architecture'. This energetic sprawl relied on the new techniques of construction, but made it painfully obvious that technical advances alone do not make for better buildings. In this period many churches were built as a kind of 'religious art' by architects who did not understand the beliefs of the congregation or the uses of the building.

The architecture of the twentieth century has no unifying style, but rather a plurality of styles. The modern freedom of choice allows a wide range of possible forms for

churches and many congregations are quite baffled when faced with the prospect of building a new church. Yet it would seem better to brave the tangles of congregational dispute than to settle for a compromise which causes no one offense but pleases no one either. Modern architecture provides scope for reinterpreting the church building as a tool for the congregation and as an emblem for the community.

The role of the church in the community is changing, too. Whilst the church is exploding in South America, Africa and South-East Asia, in the West no one is likely to call the twentieth century a particularly Christian era. But there is remarkable renewal taking place – often in unexpected ways. This renewal is bringing two things to the fore in many churches – informality

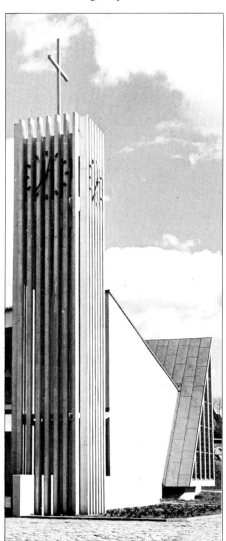

in worship, and a sense of community.
(Interestingly these seem to have been the
hallmark of the earliest Christian churches.)

Both these factors have had a direct effect
on church building. The boundary between
nave and chancel is now generally more
symbolic than physical. Open spaces are
often used for informal worship – even
including dance. Many congregations also
use their buildings for more than just
housing the weekly worship service. Some
function as community centres and schools
during the week, others provide libraries,
study rooms, lounges and space for regular
communal meals. The policy of some
congregations is that if the church grows
larger than two hundred people, another
church is begun so that close personal
contact can be maintained. Such a young

congregation might meet in a home, a school hall or a converted shop until it outgrows them.

Church building today is characterized by its great variety. Basilica types, ovals, cross plans, free form – there are few 'rules'. This willingness to experiement with form has been particularly significant for church building in the Third World. Here the traditional 'Western' forms have no roots, but local building methods and styles offer many new possibilities.

A church building is not 'the church'. But an imaginative and considered architecture can be a useful and attractive tool for the work of the church. The history of church building demonstrates that the urge to express faith through architecture is basic. The quality of church architecture depends on many factors, not least the sensitivity and dedication of the congregation concerned in assessing its role in the community. As society changes the church needs to apply the gifts and skills of its members to finding new means of expressing its life. It needs to listen, look and learn. The exploration of churches past and present can not only give pleasure but also help cultivate an alertness of what the church is called to be.

The spectacular Crystal Cathedral in California is a product of the US 'electronic church', built from $20 million donations received from vast TV audiences. It is designed in the shape of a four-cornered star to make an impressive backdrop for the TV messages delivered each Sunday from the marble pulpit.

Christians meet together to worship God in a variety of ways (CENTRE). *Purpose-designed buildings help, but they are not indispensible, as the persecuted church in the Soviet Union* (BELOW) *has shown.*

GLOSSARY

Ambulatory aisle around the chancel used for processions.

Ashlar blocks of masonry with smoothed, squared surfaces. Also called 'dressed stone'.

Ambo raised lectern, often used in medieval Italian churches, from which the Bible was read.

Apse vaulted semi-circular east end of a chancel or chapel.

Aisle side areas running parallel to the nave.

Altar table or stone slab on supports used for celebration of the Eucharist.

Arch structural support between two columns or piers made in an inverted curve.

Arcade range of arches carried on columns or piers.

Aumbry cupboard or recess used for storing cups and plates used in the Eucharist.

Bay section of wall between pillars. Generally a nave consists of a succession of bays, each with the same combination of windows and columns.

Bema raised platform in early churches, on which preacher stood to speak.

Blind (as in 'blind tracery', 'blind arcade', etc.) decorative feature applied to the surface of a wall rather than standing free.

Boss ornamental knob covering the intersection of ribs in a vault or ceiling.

Baptistry building or section of the church used for baptisms; or a baptism pool.

Basilica early style of church, consisting of a nave and two or more lower, narrower aisles.

Buttress brick or stonework built against a wall to give it support.

Capital top crowning feature of a column or pier.

Carrel (or carol) niche in a cloister, designed for a monk to sit in and work.

Chancel eastern end of a church, sometimes reserved for the clergy and choir.

Chevron Romanesque decoration in form of a zig-zag.

Chapter house assembly room in a monastery or cathedral used for discussion of business.

Choir area of the church where the services are sung.

Churrigueresque florid, highly-decorated late Baroque style, found particularly in Spain and Mexico.

Clerestory upper level of the nave wall, pierced by windows.

Cloisters external quadrangle surrounded by a covered walkway.

Column vertical load-bearing shaft with circular cross-section, usually slightly tapered.

Compound pier upright support comprised of a cluster of shafts, not necessarily attached to each other.

Corbel projecting stone block which supports a beam.

Cornice topmost decorative moulded section surmounting a column. Also any projecting moulding at the roof level of a building.

Corinthian order: see ORDER.

Crypt space beneath the main floor of a church.

Diaperwork ornamental pattern of repeated lozenges or squares.

Dogtooth early English and Norman ornamental pattern consisting of series of three-dimensional star-like shapes.

Dome vault built on a circular base.

Dressed stone see ASHLAR.

Drum round vertical wall supporting a dome.

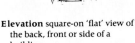

Elevation square-on 'flat' view of the back, front or side of a building.

Entablature uppermost part of the 'order' surmounting a column. Consists of cornice, frieze and architrave.

Engaged shaft see HALF SHAFT.

Facing finish material applied to the outside of a building.

Fan vault see VAULT.

Finial ornament at the tip of a spire, pinnacle or canopy.

Flamboyant late Gothic style in France, characterized by wavy lines of tracery.

Flying buttress buttress in form of arch, supporting upper portion of wall.

Gallery (or tribune) upper storey inside a church, above the aisle, open to the nave.

Gargoyle water spout projecting from a roof, often carved as a head or figure.

Groin vault see VAULT.

Grisaille stained glass with mostly white glass in small lozenge-shaped panes painted in decorative patterns.

Half shaft shaft or column partially attached to or let into a wall. Also called 'engaged shaft'.

Hall church church in which nave and aisles are about the same height.

Iconostasis screen in a Byzantine church which separates the nave from the sanctuary, usually with three doors and covered with images (icons).

Icon image of a saint, apostle or martyr used as an aid for worship of God especially in Eastern churches.

Iconoclasm opposition to the veneration of religious images.
Ionic order see ORDER.

Keystone central stone in an arch or rib.

Lancet window narrow window with a pointed arch.
Lady chapel chapel dedicated to the Virgin Mary, often at the east end of the church.
Lantern circular or polygonal tower topping a dome or roof.
Lights openings between the mullions of a window.
Lintel horizontal timber or stone beam.

Martyrion memorial or church building constructed over the grave of a martyr.
Misericord bracket on the underside of the hinged seat of the choir stall, provided for monks to lean against while standing through long services.
Mouldings contoured shaping given to projecting elements such as arches, lintels, string courses, etc.
Mullion wooden or stone framework within a window.

Narthex vestibule across the west end of a church.
Nave main middle section of the inside of a church running from the west end to the crossing.

Ogee arch see ARCH.
Order combination of columns, base, capitals, and entablature developed in ancient Rome and Greece and extensively copied in periods of classical revival. The most usual orders are Doric, Ionic and Corinthian.

Pediment gently pitched gable above a portico.
Pier solid vertical masonry support with non-circular cross-section.
Pilaster shallow pier or squared column attached to a wall.
Pinnacle small tower-like top to a spire, buttress, etc.
Piscina basin in a niche, used for washing the vessels used in the Eucharist.
Plinth projecting base of a wall.
Portico entrance in the form of a open or partially-enclosed roofed space.

Pyx container in which the bread consecrated for the Eucharist is kept. It is often elaborately carved or decorated.

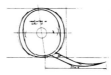

Quoins dressed stones at the corner of a building, often protruding slightly from the face of the wall.

Reredos raised decorated screen behind the communion table.
Retro-choir area behind the communion table in a cathedral.
Rib projecting stone or brickwork on a ceiling or vault, usually load-bearing.
Rood the old Saxon word for cross. Crucifix attached to a 'rood beam' and usually flanked by images of saints.
Rood screen screen below the rood separating the chancel from the nave, sometimes substantial enough to carry a 'rood loft', or gallery.

Sanctuary area around the communion table at the east end of a church.

Sedilia seats for the clergy built into the south wall of the chancel.
Spire tall conical or polygonal structure built on top of a tower.
Squinch arches placed diagonally across the corner of an intersection of walls to carry a tower, drum, or dome.
Stalls row of carved wooden or stone seats in the choir.
Steeple combination of tower and spire.
Strainer arch see ARCH.
String course projecting moulded horizontal band of stonework.

Tabernacle ornamental receptacle or recess to contain relics or the sacraments used in the Eucharist.
Transept transverse arms of a cross-shaped church.
Tribune gallery above the aisle in some cathedrals.
Triforium middle level of nave between the arcade and clerestory.
Tracery ornamental shaped stone or woodword in windows or screens.
Tympanum area between the lintel of a doorway and the arch above it, usually decorated.

Vault arched ceiling. There are several types of vault – the barrel (or tunnel) vault, the groin vault, the lierne vault and the quadrapartite vault.

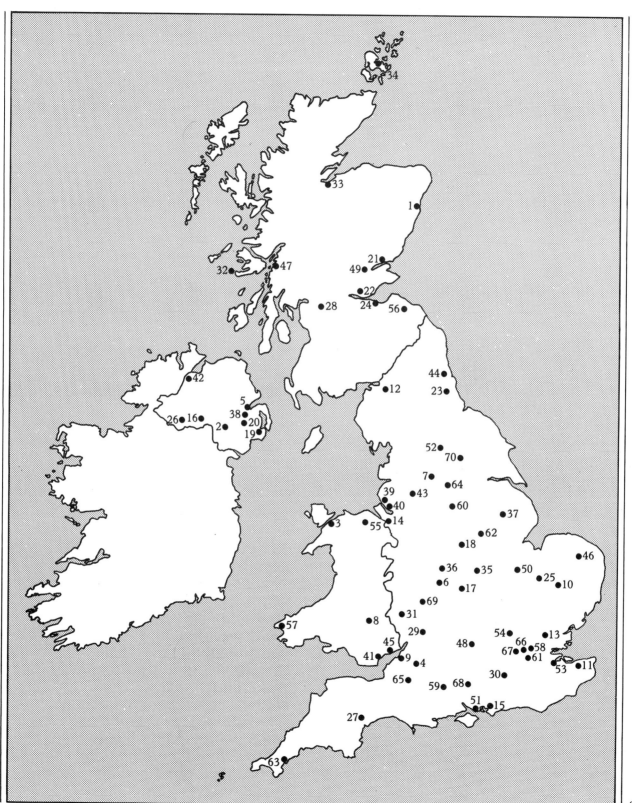

ENGLAND

Avon

BRISTOL CATHEDRAL
Holy & Undivided Trinity:
172/577733
Founded in 1140 as an Augustinian abbey, it was consecrated 25 years later. At the dissolution of the monasteries the church became in 1542, the cathedral of a new diocese.

Adjacent to the cathedral is the abbey gateway, restored in the 16th C, but retaining the original masonry in its lower courses. The central tower dates from the 15th C but the W towers are 19th C restorations.

Bristol is remarkable as being the only example in the country of a hall church. It is also remarkable for possessing two Lady Chapels, although the 'elder' adjacent to the N choir aisle was originally built as a free-standing chapel in 1215. The E Lady Chapel (1320) possesses the earliest lierne vaulting known.

The nave was rebuilt in the 16th C, but this work was interrupted by the dissolution. Unfinished and roofless, walled off from the chancel, it was allowed to become ruinous until restored in the 19th C in the style of the choir which was built between 1298 and 1330.

Other notable features are the Berkeley Chapel; the Romanesque Chapter House and the cloisters with original medieval work still in evidence.

BATH ABBEY
St Peter & St Paul:
172/756652
One of England's finest larger parish churches. It has an inspired W front showing a host of carved angels ascending into heaven up great ladders. Inside, all is light and joy born of superb proportions, huge areas of clear glass, delicate columns and magnificent vaulting.

BITTON
St Mary:
172/683694
Built on a Roman site, Saxon in origin, the church has a long Saxon nave, a late 14th C chancel, a chantry of c 1300 and probably the finest Perpendicular style tower in the region.

BRISTOL
New Room Chapel
(Methodist):
172/5973
This is the oldest licensed Methodist place of worship in England (1739), visited innumerably by John Wesley. It is a superb example of a preaching hall in classical style, and the octagonal lantern which provides light to the interior echoes the later tradition of octagonal chapels. Galleried; box pews 19th C. There is a museum collection and furnished rooms where visiting preachers would have lived and worked.

YATTON
St Mary:
172/432654
One of the most impressive churches in Avon, surmounted with a central tower crowned with a truncated stone spire. Inside there are some notable 14th and 15th C monuments, and the rarest treasure, a pall (coffin drape) made up from a late 15th C dalmatic, or open-sided ecclesiastical vestment.

Bedfordshire

COCKAYNE HATLEY
St John the Baptist:
153/256496
Medieval exterior, containing inside some of the most impressive woodwork in England, brought from Belgium in the early 19th C (except for French stalls of 1689 brought from Aulne Abbey). Other features include brasses and fine series of 13th to 18th C stained glass windows.

PAVENHAM
St Peter:
153/991559
Predominantly a 14th C exterior. Inside, there is a triumph of woodwork from different periods, consisting of every technique from marquetry to high relief.

WILLINGTON
St Lawrence:
153/106498
Historically important late Perpendicular church built, like the huge dovecote nearby, by Cardinal Wolsey's Master of Horse.

Berkshire

ASHAMPSTEAD
St Clement:
174/564767
Essentially a church of the Early English period, the chief feature is an important series of 13th C wall-paintings. These were the visual aids of the medieval church, and illustrated the stories of the Bible for the largely uneducated population.

LANGLEY MARSH
St Mary:
176/024833
The picture-book tradition of a country church containing many fine points of interest, most notable of which are the early 17th C Kederminster and Seymour transept, pew and library still serving to remind us of the importance of the church as a centre of culture and learning. The library is practically unaltered, with books, painted panelling and a heraldic over-mantel to the fireplace.

SHOTESBROOKE
St John the Baptist:
175/842771
Both inside and out, a singularly complete 14th C cruciform plan church surmounted by a lofty, elegant spire. Undoubtedly the work of one master mason with a profound sense of proportion. The interior is full of fine carved period details, including a nice sedilia, or priest's seat.

WICKHAM
St Swithin:
174/395716
To the original Saxon tower the Victorians added a 'Decorated-style' church of knapped flint with stone dressings. This hides an eccentric interior, complete with life-size papier mâché elephant heads supporting the N aisle roof, wooden angels and red and purple stained glass windows.

Buckinghamshire

AYLESBURY
St Mary:
165/817139
Mainly 13th C, large and noble with a complex plan which is actually cruciform. Much restored in the 19th C, but it has managed to retain a rare treasure – a 15th C vestment press.

CHETWODE
St Mary & St Nicholas:
165/641298
Here, in a remote spot, is the remnant of a small 13th C Augustinian priory which became the parish church in 1480. Totally 13th C it is the best example of this period in the county, enhanced only by excellent 14th C glass.

DUNTON
St Martin:
165/824244
A largely Norman church. Inside box pews; 18th C W gallery with texts and list of church dignitaries inscribed on front give the impression of rural calm.

LITTLE HAMPDEN
Ded Un:
165/849024
Architecturally reticent church with unaffected interior which contains the earliest St Christopher wall-painting in England. The timber two-storey N porch is unique in Bucks.

NORTH MARSTON
St Mary:
165/777227
Historically interesting church associated with John Schorne, rector here in the late 13th, early 14th C, who performed miraculous cures of the gout, succeeded in imprisoning the devil in a boot, and became venerated as a saint. The remains of his elaborate 14th C shrine can be seen in the S aisle. His relics, however, were removed to Windsor. The church was restored in 1855 at Queen Victoria's expense, in memory of Neild.

WEST WYCOMBE
St Laurence:
175/827949
An architectural jig-saw with fantastical overtones. Sited within an Iron Age earthwork alongside flint Dashwood mausoleum. Part medieval, partly inspirational, with unholy associations with the 18th C 'Hell-fire' Club, the tower is surmounted by an 18th C folly – a huge golden ball which seats six people inside.

WING
All Saints:
165/881226
Architecturally, probably the most important Saxon church in England, noted for its polygonal apse, vaulted crypt, aisles and for its sheer overall size. Also contains a number of good later fittings.

Cambridgeshire

ELY CATHEDRAL
Holy & Undivided Trinity:
43/542803
In 673 Etheldreda, wife of a local king, left her husband, took vows as a nun and founded a monastery for both sexes on the Isle of Ely. After Danish raiders reduced the buildings to ruin it was rebuilt in 970, but again demolished by the Normans and replaced by the present church in 1081. In 1109 the abbot was made first bishop of the see.

Architecturally, the exterior is dominated by two great octagons, which, when seen rising above the fenland mists give the whole cathedral a delicate ethereal appearance. That of the W tower is of the Decorated period with partly detached side turrets. The one topping the central tower (which collapsed in 1322) is again Decorated and is a unique and beautiful conception formed on

101

giant oak trunks, with the angles
of each stage set opposite one
another.

Inside, nothing remains of
Etheldreda's church. The nave is
late 12th C, the transepts 15th C,
and the choir is 14th C with stalls
of the same period bearing original
misericords. A shrine to St Awdry
gave our language the word
'tawdry' on account of the amount
of cheap relics sold to the pilgrims
visiting it.

Until the collapse of the tower,
the Lady Chapel had been situated
in the S aisle. It was rebuilt
adjacent to the N transept and
completed in 1349. Flooded with
light by immense windows, with
stellar vaulting and elaborately
arcaded stalls encircling its walls,
the life of the Virgin Mary is told in
sculptured scenes. Its vast span of
roof, the widest of any medieval
building, is ranked among the
richest achievements of its day, its
sculpture once brilliantly coloured
and the windows filled with
stained glass. After the
Reformation and until the present
century it was used as a parish
church.

CAMBRIDGE
Holy Sepulchre:
154/4459
Built by the powerful Knights
Templar's, a quasi-military
religious order, originally
established to provide protection
to pilgrims and crusaders in the
Holy Land. One of only four of
their once-numerous distinctive
round churches remaining in
England.

NORTHBOROUGH
St Andrew:
142/154078
This is the surviving fragment of a
much larger church. Mostly 12th
and 13th C work. Historical
association with Cromwell (his
wife is buried here), as is the wife
of John Clare, Northants peasant-
poet.

PEAKIRK
St Pega:
142/168066
Developed from the site of the cell
of St Pega into a much-restored
medieval chapel, now part of a
convent. Norman bell-tower and
14th C wall-paintings.

RAMSEY
St Thomas of Canterbury:
142/293856
Part of the monastic abbey built
originally as a 'hospitium' to care
for the sick and infirm; the
presence of a 13th C font indicates
that it was probably always a
parish church, too. Predominantly
12th C.

SWAFFHAM PRIOR
St Mary & St Cyriac:
154/568639
One of the few parishes in England
where two churches coexist in one
graveyard. Unfortunately one is
partially ruined, and both are in
the care of the RCF.

Cheshire

CHESTER CATHEDRAL
Christ & the Blessed Virgin
Mary:
117/406665
The first church at Chester was
built in 907 to shelter the relics of a
royal nun, St Werburgh. It was
administered at this time by a
college of priests, but the Normans
soon replaced them with
Benedictine monks who
immediately demolished the
Saxon church. The monks,
however, continued to honour the
parochial responsibilities
established during the original
foundation, and the S aisle of the
nave was set aside as the church of
Chester, an arrangement which
persisted into the 14th C.

In 1540 the monastery was
dissolved, but the church
remained to become the cathedral
of a new diocese, although from
the 17th to the 19th C the S
transept served as the parish
church, too.

The surviving church was
almost completely rebuilt between
the 13th and 16th C but remnants
of the Norman edifice can still be
seen. Of the final phase of
construction, the W front of the
early 1500s remains, as does the
upper portion of the central tower.
Twin W towers, as at Lichfield,
were planned but never realized,
but their ground storeys were
erected. A SW porch was added in
1508. The remains of monastic
buildings are extensive, and the S
walk of the cloisters contains the
carrels or cubicles where the
monks studied.

Internally, the earliest portion of
the church is the rugged arch and
Romanesque triforium preserved
in the N transept. What is now the
baptistry dates from the 12th C.
The work of the 14th C is most
apparent and encompasses the
choir with its fine stalls and
magnificent misericords dating
from 1390, the S arcade, and parts
of the S transept. The N arcade of
the nave and clerestory windows
are of the 15th and 16th C and the
fine timber roof is early 16th C
also.

The cathedral was further
restored in later centuries.

BADDILEY
St Michael:
118/605504
A 'cosy' church with half-timbered
chancel and 17th C brick nave
encasing an earlier structure.
Famous for its tympanum, one of
the most interesting in England
which is 20ft square and painted
with the Creed, Commandments,
Lord's Prayer and heraldic arms,
dated 1663.

CHOLMONDELEY
St Nicholas:
117/545516
A cruciform-planned private
chapel to the nearby castle. The
family pew or state gallery has

cushions made from robes worn at
the coronation of William IV.

CONGLETON
St Peter:
118/859627
An 18th C town church with
contemporary glass, galleries, brass
candelabrum, font and altar rails.
Unique to the county, the pulpit is
centrally placed in front of the
altar in order to satisfy the
liturgical fashion of the period for
immense sermons.

LOWER PEOVER
St Oswald:
118/744743
Despite restoration, an excellent
example of a timber-built church,
with tower of stone. Inside, the
atmosphere is still 'medieval' and
some of the box pews have their
lower halves fixed to retain the
rushes – once the standard floor
covering of parish churches and
houses in certain parts of the
country. The old church custom of
'rush bearing' stems from the
annual changing of these reeds.

MOBBERLEY
St Wilfrid:
109/802971
A typical E Cheshire medieval
church. The glory here is the
magnificent rood screen of 1500
with a rood ceilure overhead,
painted and adorned to represent
heaven above the 'rood' or great
crucifix which once stood below.

Cleveland

KIRKLEATHAM
St Cuthbert:
93/594218
Perhaps the most interesting
church building in this
administrative county. A church
and attached mausoleum of
predominantly 18th C work.
External details include
Chippendale Gothic door to the
octagonal Baroque Turner
mausoleum. Inside dominated by
rows of Tuscan columns on
pedestals, but despite restoration,
there is a wealth of original
furniture including 14th C parish
chest which would have housed all
the important documents of the
church.

MARTON
St Cuthbert:
93/516157
Historically important as the
baptism church of Capt. James
Cook, RN, although since then it
has been totally rebuilt (1843).

STOCKTON-ON-TEES
St Thomas:
93/444186
Light in an otherwise drab
landscape; a stately Classical
building of 1710–12 in which
Wren had a hand in the design.
The imposing pulpit was once part

of a three-decker, and among the
fine woodwork one should note,
for interest, the 18th C altar and
rails carved from the wood of Capt.
Cook's ship, *Endeavour*.

UPLEATHAM
St Andrew:
94/636194
The surviving W part of the nave
of a large Norman church often
mistaken for a complete church
and consequently, occasionally
referred to incorrectly, as the
smallest church in England. The
tower is 17th C.

Cornwall

TRURO CATHEDRAL
St Mary:
204/826449
In Saxon times, Cornwall had a
cathedral at St Germans, but
Edward the Confessor united the
diocese with that of Exeter.

The present diocese was formed
in 1887 and the foundation stone
of the cathedral laid three years
later. The church was completed in
1910, and incorporates the parish
church of St Mary in part. Its
overall style is imitation Gothic.

Apart from the rebuilding of St
Paul's, this was the first cathedral
to be erected since the
Reformation. Designed by John L.
Pearson, it was finished after his
death by his son, F.L. Pearson.

Internally, the majority of
fittings are modern, only the N
aisle is medieval, and glass of this
century reflects the Christian
concerns of the times – work,
mission and church history.

ALTARNUM
St Nonna:
201/223813
Shadowed by one of the loftiest
towers in Cornwall, this
Perpendicular church contains a
fine display of medieval art, in
particular the rood screen which
spans the chancel and aisles. Early
17th C panels depict the Holy
Communion and the Crucifixion.

LANLIVERY
St Brevita:
200/080591
As with many Cornish churches,
an unusual dedication, here to St
Brevita. One of the great churches
of the county, re-fashioned in the
15th C. There is a nice ringers'
rhyme board.

LINKINHORNE
St Melor:
201/319736
Built from local granite. Inside,
there is a wagon roof typical of the
SW and a wall-painting showing
the Works of Mercy. A holy well,
of late medieval structure, stands
in a nearby field.

ST ENDELLION
St Endelienta:
200/997787
An isolated prebendal or 'Chapter' church surrounded by the low slate houses of the prebendaries, which seem to have survived all Reformations.

Cumbria

CARLISLE CATHEDRAL
Holy & Undivided Trinity:
85/399559
Despite being set in a traditionally ancient ecclesiastical stronghold, it was not until the 12th C that the first church was built here. In 1123 an Augustinian priory was founded, and ten years later it was made the seat of a bishopric.

Between the Middle Ages and the 17th C, the city was continually engulfed in border wars, and the cathedral bears witness to a history of troubled times. In the 13th and 14th C fire partially destroyed the church. In the war against Scotland the monastic buildings were wantonly demolished, and in the Jacobite rising the church served as a prison on which many of the inmates left their mark.

Architecturally, the church might be considered unprepossessing. The Norman work is much altered and marred, the E window is ill-aligned within the gable and the triforium is misshapen due to subsidence while building. But in balance there is a fine W window with original glass in part, and the backs of the stalls are decorated with 15th C paintings depicting the lives of St Antony, St Cuthbert and St Augustine. The capitals of the pillars have delightful sculptures representing the months of the year.

The remains of the monastic buildings are on the S side of the church. The Fratery was erected in 1350, but rebuilt the following century. It has a W window of notable design and a wall pulpit. A tower refuge, the upper floor of which was the prior's lodging, has massive walls and was probably intended as a protective shelter against Scottish raiders.

APPLEBY-IN-WESTMORLAND
St Lawrence:
91/684205
An Early English style church with Perpendicular overtones. Among a number of fine fittings, it contains the tomb of Lady Anne Clifford, who restored this (1655) and numerous other churches in the area. It also has probably the oldest working organ in England (c1542), brought here from Carlisle cathedral in the late 17th C.

BURGH-BY-SANDS
St Michael:
85/328591
Built largely of stone from Hadrian's Wall, on which line it stands. In the vicinity is a monument to Edward I who died in camp on Burgh Marsh 1307.

CROSTHWAITE
St Kentigern:
97/446912
Built on an ancient site, the present church is mostly 16th C, but restored. Contains many curiosities: an 18th C pitch-pipe, a conductor's baton, and old rhymes admonishing bell-ringers not to swear, or ring in spurs or hats. Its greatest treasure must be the series of medieval consecration crosses, 12 outside and 9 inside; in such numbers, unique to this church.

GRASMERE
St Oswald:
90/336074
Of 11th, 13th and 17th C date. Its most notable architectural feature is a continuous two-storey arcade. Wordsworth and members of his family are buried here.

ISEL
St Michael:
89/163333
A largely Norman church near to a medieval fortified hall. On the 15th C window, three sundials mark the monastic hours, and on one of the pre-Norman crosses is a rare three-armed symbol, a triskele, one of the earlier Christian devices.

Derbyshire

DERBY CATHEDRAL
All Saints:
128/353365
The bishopric was formed in 1927, the parish church being adopted as the cathedral. Designed by James Gibbs, it was built in 1723. It was extended eastwards in the 1960s to form a new sanctuary.

The tower is early 16th C and is the sole remnant of the original church which, it is said, was otherwise totally demolished overnight by a rector who was in dispute with the city corporation.

Internally, features of merit include an 18th C ironwork screen bounding the sanctuary, embellished by the heraldic arms of the House of Hanover and made locally by Robert Bakewell; and a colourful tomb commemorating Bess of Hardwick, who died in 1607 having outlived four husbands and given birth to the founder of the Devonshire family.

BREADSALL
All Saints:
128/371398
Predominantly 13th and 14th C, but internally heavily restored after a fire in 1915 started by Suffragettes. Possibly the finest steeple in the county.

DALE ABBEY
All Saints:
129/436386
Near to the site of 12th C abbey, with a hermitage close by. Miniscule church with farmhouse under one roof. 17th C furnishings – 'cupboard' altar; pulpit of 1634; reading desk and box pews. Pleasant 14th C mural of the Visitation.

DERBY
St Mary's Chapel, Bridge Gate:
128/3536
One of only five 'bridge' chapels to survive in England. Built 14th C to serve the needs of itinerants.

MELBOURNE
St Michael & St Mary:
128/389250
Huge and ambitious Norman church c1130, remnant of a once important abbey in a town that was later depopulated. Twin W and central towers; stone-vaulted narthex; circular apses to chancel and aisles. Internally, similar to St Bartholomew-the-Great, London, with ponderous round inscribed pillars; triforium with clerestory and processional way all round.

REPTON
St Wystan:
128/303272
Originally a Saxon foundation, the chancel and crypt date from this period. It has all styles of architecture from 10th to 15th C.

Devon

EXETER CATHEDRAL
St Peter:
192/921926
Originally, the cathedral of Devon was centred at Crediton, but as a result of continuous attack by pirates, Edward the Confessor had the bishopric attached to Exeter and given into the charge of secular canons. It is probable that the site of the present cathedral was occupied by a monastery in 670, of which the church was rebuilt in 932 and again in 1019 after destruction by Danish raiders.

In the reign of William I, it was decided to rebuild the church on a larger scale and the completed building was consecrated in 1133. This church in turn was almost entirely rebuilt in the following two centuries.

The N and S towers were erected in 1133, and apart from Norman buttresses to the N wall of the nave are the only relics of the Romanesque edifice.

The W front, with its array of 13th C statues, all once brilliantly coloured and backed by gilded niches, is much defaced and reflects little of its former majesty.

Inside, the great chu... unusual in having no c... tower, is notable for bei... single style of architectu... wholly dating from the ... ...th C. It is recorded that a scribe was engaged to write out 800 indulgences in 1349 to raise money for the work.

BRANSCOMBE
St Winifred:
192/196885
Isolated church of architectural importance. Work from the 11th to 16th C. Inside, the woodwork is worth close inspection, especially the Elizabethan W gallery, the altar rails enclosing altar on four sides, and the magnificent three-decker pulpit – rare in Devon.

BUCKLAND MONACHORUM
St Andrew:
201/491683
Noble 15th and 16th C church associated with Francis Drake, whose monument can be seen here.

CHITTLEHAMPTON
St Urith:
180/636256
Dedicated to local saint, murdered c700 by pagan villagers. She is buried in the church of ancient date. Her holy well lies at the E end of village.

OTTERY ST MARY
St Mary:
192/098956
Perhaps the county's most architecturally important church. Closely modelled on Exeter cathedral, the interior is impressive and of particular note is the vaulting, the most spectacular being that in the Dorset aisle of c1520 which is a fan-vault with pendants. Externally, a fine series of consecration crosses.

SAMPFORD COURTENAY
St Andrew:
191/633013
Mainly 16th C work, inside, simple, light and spacious. This village was the hatching ground for the Prayer Book Rebellion of 1549 which began and ended here.

Dorset

BRIDPORT
Chapel (Quaker):
193/4692
Typical of the origins of so many Quaker meeting houses, this chapel was first a barn, adopted to its present use following a visit to the town by George Fox in 1655. As with buildings of this religious group, the exterior is unremarkable, indeed, hardly recognizable as a chapel. This was often deliberately done in order to avoid persecution. Internally, all is plain and simple, yet managing to appear rich; benches to form three sides of a square and a gallery are

all that mark this as a building for worship.

HILTON
All Saints:
194/782029
An example of a Dorset county church which could well have been built for the pages of a Hardy novel. Mainly late Gothic its features include a fine range of 15th C windows from Milton Abbey, now destroyed, and 12 panels with early 16th C figure paintings of the Apostles from the same source.

LONGBURTON
St James:
194/648127
Predominantly Perpendicular, the tower Early English with a 13th C upper stage. Noted for its monuments, including ancestors of Sir Winston Churchill.

WHITCHURCH CANONICORUM
St Candida & Holy Cross:
193/396955
An Early English building for the most part, unique in this country in that it retains relics of its patroness in a 13th C shrine. As for the rest, good monuments in a spacious and light church.

WIMBORNE MINSTER
St Cuthberga:
195/009999
Cruciform church, formerly collegiate and the only instance of a two-towered church in the county. Full of medieval interest, but of especial note are the coloured tower ceilings and the vaulted crypt, simple and moving.

County Durham

DURHAM CATHEDRAL
Church of Christ & the Blessed Virgin Mary:
88/273421
The first church here was a mean and lowly shelter, erected in 995 to house the body of St Cuthbert, a revered saint, which had been carried from the vulnerable monastery of Lindisfarne for safety, along with the head of St Oswald and the fabled Lindisfarne Gospels.

The Normans despised the humble Saxon church and replaced it with a grand stone edifice which has survived almost intact to become today the most wholly Romanesque church in the country. The shrine of St Cuthbert, administered by Benedictine monks, became one of the most visited in England, and it is said that some 7,000 masses were intoned annually.

The church also sheltered the remains of Bede, the 8th C monk/historian, which were stolen from the monastery of Jarrow and presented to Durham.

Durham was one of only 20 British churches able to give sanctuary, and the medieval sanctuary knocker on the NW door is among the unique possessions of the church. The watching chambers above, however, were destroyed by Wyatt in a restoration. Sanctuary – mostly to homicides – was given for 37 days on condition the person carried no weapon and wore a special badge; an oath to abjure the realm was then taken and, holding a white cross, he was permitted to travel to the nearest port.

Architecturally the church is Norman, the nave space dominated by huge cylindrical pillars carved with typical geometrical designs. Externally, the building is dominated by the great central tower first built in 1262, but restored in the 14th C due to severe lightning damage. The noble W towers, however, are wholly 12th C.

The vaulting in Durham is some of the earliest known, and can be seen in the 12th C aisles, choir and crossing, and that in the nave is quite remarkable.

Another notable feature of the church is the galilee (covered porchway at the W end) of spacious proportions, which shelters the now empty tomb of Bede, and bears on one of its walls a magnificent 12th C painting of Cuthbert.

The monastic buildings are approached through the S transept with its clock in a 15th C case with a thistle emblem (said to have caused its preservation when the church was used as a prison in 1650 for 4,000 starving Scots captured at the battle of Dunbar). The cloisters survive, the dormitory of 1404 retains its original roof, and the prior's kitchen still serves the deanery today.

BRANCEPTH
St Brandon:
93/225377
Built between the 12th and 17th C, it is especially noted for its woodwork, given by John Cosin, rector here from 1626 and later Bishop of Durham. This includes a magnificent chancel screen, pews, pulpit, ceilings, choir stalls and more, all of which carry fine detail. Fragments of medieval rood screen.

CHESTER-LE-STREET
St Mary & St Cuthbert:
88/276514
Practically engulfed by 20th C development, it is recognizable by curious tower with octagonal storey and capped with 14th C spire. Of various dates, it possesses an Anchorite's cell with squint to afford the occupant a view of the altar.

ESCOMBE
Ded Un:
92/189301
A simple, untouched Saxon church of majestic beauty.

Inscribed stone from Roman fort at Binchester built into N wall, and an interesting sundial can be seen above the porch. Text-book long-and-short work as well as Roman masonry.

SEAHAM
St Mary the Virgin:
88/426494
Like so many Co. Durham churches of ancient origin, Roman masonry incorporated. Simple almost austere architecture. Nice double piscina with a mysterious design of priest's hand raised in blessing is cut into its arch. Parish registers record Lord Byron's marriage.

Essex

CHELMSFORD CATHEDRAL
St Mary, St Peter & St Cedd:
167/708069
On the formation of the diocese in 1914, the parish church became the cathedral.

Like many churches of Essex, the building is predominantly flint. It was rebuilt by the townspeople during the 15th C, of which the tower, crowned today by an 18th C spire, is almost the only remnant.

The 15th C porch is patterned with flints and has a carved medieval ceiling, two-storied. The upper chamber houses a library.

Internally, the nave is a rebuild following collapse, and little of its previous architecture has survived the 19th C restoration. The roof has gilded corbel figures. Interestingly, two of the W pillars have been hollowed out, apparently to provide cupboards.

On the N side is the brilliantly coloured Tudor tomb of the Mildmay family, the father with eight sons facing the mother with her nine daughters.

BRADWELL-ON-SEA
St Peter-on-the-wall:
168/004069
One of the oldest churches in the county, still retaining its 7th C nave practically untouched from the original building of c654, erected by St Cedd. Materials mostly taken from the ancient Roman fort of Othona, on the site of which the church is reputed to stand.

COPFORD GREEN
St Michael & All Angels:
168/936226
As Pickering is to Yorkshire, so Copford is to Essex. The whole of this 12th C church interior is a blaze of coloured wall-paintings, the finest of which is the beautiful depiction of Christ in Majesty on the half-domed vault over the apse. In the S aisle (c1300) are some of the oldest medieval bricks in the country.

GREENSTED-JUXTA-ONGAR
St Andrew:
167/539030
Despite restorations, this church remains one of the most important in England – the only surviving example of what was originally a timber Saxon church. Unfortunately all that remains of the Saxon building are the nave walls of huge split oak logs.

HADSTOCK
St Botolph:
154/558446
Probably the Minster erected by Canute in 1020 to commemorate his victory over Edmund Ironside at Assendum. A remarkable Saxon cruciform church entered through a S door which must be one of the oldest in the country.

NEWPORT
St Mary the Virgin:
154/521341
A large town church of 13th to 16th C work. Among its furnishings is an unusual and important 13th C portable altar in the form of a chest, the lid of which opens to form a reredos with early paintings.

STEBBING
St Mary the Virgin:
167/664240
Predominantly 14th C full of interest. Good timber roof, even in a county renowned for its timbered churches; fine stone chancel screen; and a rare feature, in the chancel a pulley block for drawing the lentern veil.

Gloucestershire

GLOUCESTER CATHEDRAL
Holy & Indivisible Trinity:
162/829188
The cathedral occupies the site of a 7th C abbey which was rebuilt during the reign of Canute. A third rebuilding of 1089 was interrupted by fire and not completed until 1160. Two hundred years later the monks provided a burial place for Edward II after three other cathedrals had refused. The murdered king was popularly accepted as a saint and multitudes of pilgrims provided immense wealth to the Gloucester monastery, the fruit of which gave rise to the birth of Perpendicular architecture. In 1540 the monastery was dissolved and the church became a cathedral.

Architecturally, the W front dates from 1420 when the original W towers were demolished. The central tower was rebuilt in 1450.

The nave was completed in 1160, its Romanesque arches supported by immense columns. The vaulting dates from the following century, but the W bays were rebuilt in 1420 and the clerestory windows added.

The S transept is reputedly the

birthplace of Perpendicular architecture.

The E window of the choir is of unequalled majesty, and retains its original glass commemorating those who fought at the battle of Crecy. It is wider than the choir, and the walls are bayed out to receive it. The choir itself possibly marks the highest achievement of architecture, combining an appearance of weightlessness with superb unity of style for which architects of the medieval period continually strived.

Of the monastic buildings, the cloisters are unusually situated N of the nave, and are of outstanding magnificence, with fan-vaulting of unparalleled splendour. The north walk has a finely preserved lavatorium and a recess for towels. In the W walk are the carrels or study cubicles.

It was from Gloucester that William the Conqueror ordered the compilation of the Domesday Book completed in 1086.

ASHLEWORTH
St Andrew & St Bartholomew:
162/819252
Notable church with 14th C spire. In its setting near the tithe barn and court house, it admirably demonstrates the church's place within the local community.

CIRENCESTER
St John the Baptist:
163/023021
In a county with remarkable 'wool' churches, this must be the most remarkable of them all, and is perhaps the most beautiful Perpendicular church in England. Visually exciting and full of medieval fittings. The three-storey porch was once the town hall and is noted for its two-storey oriel window.

DEERHURST
St Mary:
150/871299
Originally founded in the 8th C as an Anglo-Saxon monastery, it was rebuilt in the 10th C after the Vikings had left it in ruins. Internally one is struck by the immense height. Curious double triangular-headed windows open high up from the tower into the nave. Sanctuary set out in 17th C manner. Nearby is a chapel erected by Earl Odda in 1056.

Hampshire

WINCHESTER CATHEDRAL
Holy Trinity, St Peter, St Paul & St Swithin:
185/483293
A church was erected here in 645 and enlarged in the 10th C. It was rebuilt between 1079 and 1093 and attained the grandeur of its present form between 1346 and 1404 when William of Wykeham was bishop.

At one time the capital of England, Winchester saw the coronation of both Richard I and William I.

Externally, the W front is 14th C. The central tower is Norman, rebuilt in the 12th C after a collapse in 1107. The N transept has a walled-up doorway which once admitted pilgrims to St Swithin's shrine. Adjacent to the S transept are the remains of the Chapter House which was demolished in the 17th C.

Inside, the church is predominantly 14th C which includes the nave and the choir. The choir was completed before the nave, and is flanked by 16th C screens on which rest mortuary chests containing the bones of Saxon kings. The magnificent choir stalls were carved in 1308.

The shrine of Bishop Swithin, who died in 862, once stood beyond the altar, attracting great numbers of pilgrims. He had left instructions that he was to be buried outside the church and when his body was transferred to the interior in 971, the state of the weather for a number of days afterwards gave rise to the story that if it rains on St Swithin's day, forty more rainy days will follow.

No other cathedral possesses so rich a collection of chantry chapels. N and S of the high altar are those of Bishop Gardiner (1555) and Bishop Fox (1528). N and S of the Lady Chapel are the chantries of Bishop Wayneflete (1486) and Cardinal Beaufort (1447). East of this is the chantry of Bishop Langton (1501). The S side of the nave has the chantry of Bishop Edington.

BEAULIEU
Blessed Virgin and Child:
196/388026
Established in the refectory of the Cistercian abbey. It still retains the monastic reader's desk approached through the thickness of the wall by a graceful arcaded stair.

BREAMORE
St Mary:
185/154189
An architecturally important church c1000. Originally cruciform, it is made up of and contains much text-book work. Nice timber roof often overlooked in favour of other features, and a delightful array of hatchments in the tower crossing. Inscription over the S transept archway reads 'Here the Covenant becomes Manifest to Thee'.

ELLINGHAM
St Mary:
195/144084
An 18th C rustic simplicity which hides an interior of complex design and rare treasures. Medieval screen with hour-glass; 16th C tympanum with painted Decalogue, texts and Royal Arms. At W end against W door a fine reredos by Grindling Gibbons surrounds Italian painting. Externally, S porch carries an

interesting and huge blue and gold painted sundial.

SELBORNE
St Mary:
186/742337
Of Norman Transition and Early English date, it was restored by the great-nephew of Gilbert White, naturalist and diarist, who is buried in the churchyard under a humble stone inscribed 'GW 1793'.

Herefordshire and Worcestershire

HEREFORD CATHEDRAL
The Blessed Virgin Mary & St Ethelbert:
149/510397
The bishopric of Hereford is reputed to have been in existence in 544, and the bishop to have been among those members of the church who held conference with St Augustine on the banks of the Severn a few years after his arrival in Kent.

Certainly a church and see are documented in the 7th C and by 825 an 'admirable stone church' had been erected. In it were preserved the relics of King Ethelbert of East Anglia. A new building was built in 1055, but gutted shortly afterwards by Welsh raiders. This was restored by the Normans in 1080, and enlarged the following century.

In 1282 the secular canons who cared for the church obtained the canonization of their bishop, Thomas Cantelope, who died at Rome and whose chaplain had thoughtfully boiled the corpse and brought the bones back to England. Thomas Cantelope, who had been treasurer of England, was the last Englishman to be canonized by the pope before the Reformation.

After a long period of neglect following ill-treatment of the church by Cromwellians, it was restored in the 18th C – unfortunately not very successfully – and it was at this time that two tons of ancient brasses were shamefully sold off.

The cathedral's most precious possession, however, has remained intact: a medieval chained library of 5,000 books, a collection begun in early Norman times.

WORCESTER CATHEDRAL
Christ & the Blessed Virgin Mary:
150/849546
There was a bishopric here in the 7th C and it is said that Oswald, who was bishop from 983, built a cathedral with 28 altars. Edward the Confessor elected Wulfstan to the see on Oswald's death. He was the only bishop to retain his cathedra after the Conquest, and

assisted at the coronation. Oswald's cathedral had been burned by the Danes in 1041, and had since remained in a state of ruins. Wulfstan now began a new building. Fires did much damage in 1113 and 1202. After the battle of Worcester, Cromwell's army used the church as a prison and was responsible for much vandalism. Consequently, much of the church is a 19th C restoration.

The central tower of the Norman church collapsed in 1175, and the present majestic tower was erected in 1370. The spacious N porch is of the late 14th C.

Like Canterbury, of particular note is the crypt belonging to Wulfstan's church. And, although partially filled now by blocks and rubble to provide support for the 14th C building, the forest of simple Romanesque pillars is attractive.

BESFORD
St Peter:
150/911447
Slightly restored in 1880, it remains for the most a 14th C church and has the distinction of being the only timber-framed church in the county. 14th C bells and a complete rood loft. 16th C triptych with painted figures.

BREDWARDINE
St Andrew:
149/334445
Predominantly Norman, with a Georgian tower. Associated with Francis Kilvert, the famous diarist, who was rector here from 1877 until his death in 1879.

TYBERTON
St Mary:
149/380399
Originally Norman, rebuilt 1720 in brick with Classical tower. Its most noted feature is the beautiful early 18th C reredos carved with the symbols of the passion, in a spirit of mysticism unusual for the period.

Hertfordshire

ST ALBANS ABBEY
St Alban:
166/145071
Originally founded as an abbey in 793, the church was subsequently rebuilt in 1115 by the Normans and re-dedicated. It grew into the richest monastic house in the country. Following the dissolution, it was sold to the town for the sum of £400. At the time, Henry VIII proposed that it should become the cathedral of a new diocese, but it was not until 1877 that the church was raised to cathedral status and a diocese formed.

The central tower was built in Roman brick from the nearby Verulamium. The W end collapsed in 1323 and the flanking towers were demolished to provide stone for rebuilding. By the 19th C, however, it had become ruinous, and it was only through the wealthy benefaction of Lord Grimthorpe that extensive restoration was possible, including the rebuilding of the W front. The St Matthew sculpture in the porch is his portrait.

The only remains of the domestic buildings of this once great abbey are the arcading of the N wall of the cloister and the massive 14th C gateway which until the 19th C was used as a prison.

Internally, the earliest work from the first church can be seen in the crossing, parts of the transepts, and a wall on the N side to which the 12th C W bays, triforium and clerestory is joined. The rest of the cathedral is mostly 13th and 15th C work.

The base of St Alban's shrine was recovered in the 19th C from the rubble filling the E arches of the presbytery, and was reassembled from 2,000 fragments. Though only partially rebuilt, it provides a fine impression of its medieval appearance. This preserved stone base is carved with scenes of St Alban's martyrdom and still retains traces of medieval colouring. N of the shrine stands the watching chamber of 1400, with cupboards for relics beneath, from which monks kept sentinel as the streams of pilgrims walked in procession past the shrine.

ANSTEY
St George:
167/404328
A deceptive building, giving the impression of being larger than it actually is. Of many periods, Transitional central tower c1200; 16th C stalls and misericords in a 13th C chancel, as are the transepts, with their squints to afford a view of the altar; and the rest comprises of 14th and 15th C work.

AYOT ST LAWRENCE
St Lawrence:
166/195169
Set as a focal point in a parkland view, the old parish church stands in ruins next to the new, a Greek temple with flanking pavilions and linking screens designed by Revet in 1778–79. Internally, however, the detail is Roman classical tempered to Anglican 18th C. The E end is a coffered apse.

HITCHIN
St Mary:
166/185291
A sumptuous church which serves to exaggerate the town's declining fortunes. Architecturally 12th – 15th C with a rich interior full of monuments, woodwork and brasses. Spectacular two-storey S porch undoubtedly built by a merchant.

TRING
New Mill Chapel (Baptist):
165/923113
A beautiful red-brick chapel and schoolhouse set in a spacious graveyard. Well worth a visit to savour the contemplative atmosphere of the unrestored early 1800s interior.

WARE
St Mary:
166/356145
Mainly 14th and 15th C periods, its most notable features are the transepts, unusual in being carried to full nave height and embellished with clerestories. Another fine feature is the octagonal font of c1380, the most elaborate in Herts.

Humberside

ALDBROUGH
St Bartholomew:
107/244387
One of the few churches retaining an inscribed Anglo-Saxon sundial, which reads 'Ulf who ordered this church to be built for his own and Gunware's souls.' Also of note, a late 14th C military effigy.

APPLEBY
St Bartholomew:
112/954152
Largely rebuilt in 1800, when fragments of masonry from Thornholme Priory were incorporated. Of considerable interest are the remains of an old church custom, traces of funeral blacking applied to the interior walls on the death of a notable parish personage, in this case, a former Lord St Oswald.

BOTTESFORD
St Peter's Chains:
112/899070
An Early English church with a rare dedication. The lancet windows of the chancel are said to be the longest in any parish church in England. The N transept, formerly known as the Morley choir, was used for a considerable period as the burial place of the ancient Catholic family of that name.

GOODMANHAM
All Saints:
106/890431
Reputed to occupy the site of a pagan temple which Bede tells us was destroyed by Coifi, the chief priest, after his conversion to Christianity in 627. The most ornate font in the area is here, probably made on the eve of the Reformation and inscribed 'with owt baptysm no soull ma be saved'.

SWINE
St Mary:
107/134358
Formed out of the aisled chancel of a cruciform church which was part of a Cistercian nunnery. Beautiful assembly of alabaster effigal tombs and 16th C screenwork and misericord stalls to assist the clergy to stand during the long medieval church services.

Isle of Wight

PORTSMOUTH CATHEDRAL
St Thomas of Canterbury:
196/639005
The first church was erected at the end of the 12th C and given into the charge of Augustinian canons. Its tower was used as a naval watch-tower, and consequently suffered on account of this secular occupation, especially during the Civil War. Ultimately, both nave and tower had to be rebuilt.

The church became the cathedral of a new diocese in 1927. Ambitious plans to enlarge it were instigated which still have not been completed.

Of the original foundation of 1196, the Lady Chapel to the N has survived, and the sanctuary and Martyrs Chapel on the S. The choir is 17th C and formed the nave of the 18th C church. The rest is comparatively modern.

Some of the more interesting objects to be seen include a della Robbia Madonna of 1500; the ship weathervane which stood on the apex of the cupola (1703) and a fragment of the flag of Lord Nelson's *Victory*.

CARISBROOKE
St Mary:
196/485883
Overshadowed by the castle, the church, with its stately Perpendicular W tower, has been described as 'the most important ecclesiastical building in the Island'. It was originally monastic, while simultaneously parochial, but the priory was suppressed in 1414 and none of the conventual buildings have survived. The church suffered the loss of its chancel in c1565.

SHORWELL
St Peter:
196/457830
An almost unrestored wholly Perpendicular church with an extraordinary collection of poppy-headed pews. There is also an important wall-painting of St Christopher, depicting several episodes in the life of the saint.

WHIPPINGHAM
St Mildred:
196/511936
A 'royal' church, in the sense that it was much patronized by Queen Victoria and the then royal family, who gave a number of sumptuous

fittings. Architecturally Germanic Gothic and partly designed by Prince Albert. There are various memorials to members of the royal family.

Kent

CANTERBURY CATHEDRAL
Church of Christ:
179/151578
In 597 St Augustine landed in Kent, baptized King Ethelbert, and erected the first cathedral. This was an oblong building with a crypt, an apse at either end, and N and S towers, beneath one of which was the entrance porch. In 741 a detached baptistry was added.

By 1067, however, the church had become ruined through neglect and fire. The Norman Archbishop Lanfranc had it rebuilt on more traditional lines to the obviously Roman influenced previous building. This included a central tower, transepts, nave and twin W towers. Lanfranc placed it in the charge of Benedictine monks.

In the following century the nave was rebuilt on a greater scale and the Norman choir, destroyed by fire in 1174, was re-erected early in the following century to a lavish design to contain the relics of the murdered Archbishop Thomas à Becket. The present nave, set at a slight angle to the choir, was built 200 years later. The ascending levels as it progresses from nave to the E corona chapel are an outstanding feature of the cathedral.

Architecturally, the church is dominated by the great 15th C central tower known as 'Bell Harry' which is one of the finest in the country.

The eastern termination of the church is of particular interest, forming a chevet with the corona chapel as its eastern chapel in contrast to the normal square end of the English cathedral.

Inside, there is much of note, as is expected in a church of such antiquity and such prominence, but in particular Canterbury possesses the largest Norman crypt in the world, a relic of the 12th C building. The capitals of the pillars, finely carved with beasts, are exceptional. In 1952 mural paintings dating from the 12th C were discovered in the crypt chapel of St Gabriel, and these have been beautifully restored.

ROCHESTER CATHEDRAL
Christ & the Blessed Virgin Mary:
178/743685
The cathedral was founded by St Augustine in 604. Its site near the river made it an inevitable target for Danish raids, and the Normans found it ruinous. Bishop Gundulph rebuilt the church in 1080, but it was much damaged by

fires in the 12th C. The 14th C rebuilding was prevented by lack of funds. The church suffered from the vandalism of the Puritans, but most of all at the hands of the 18th and 19th C restorers.

Architecturally, the exterior is much altered and only the W front of 1130 survives in any complete form. Flanking the ornately sculptured W entrance are two statues to Henry I and his queen, which are reputedly the oldest in the country. On the N side of the church, between the two transepts, is a tower of 1080, which was probably built as a defense against Danish raiders.

Inside, the nave is the oldest in England, dating from the late 11th and early 12th C. The triforium has the earliest pointed arches in the country. The clerestory was added in the 15th C. A mural painting representing St Christopher is to be seen on a S pillar. Further mural decorations of the 14th C can be seen in the choir, and on the N side is a painted medieval 'Wheel of Fortune'.

The crypt belongs partially to Gundulph's church, the W end dates from 1080, the E is 13th C. On the piers are some medieval graffiti.

BROOKLAND
St Augustine:
189/989258
The most remarkable architectural feature of this mainly 13th C church is the detached timber belfry, octagonal in plan, with three stages stacked on one another like cones, and shingled from top to bottom. Unrestored interior with the most exquisite 12th C lead font.

CANTERBURY
St Martin:
179/1557
Possibly the oldest parish church in England, for it was here that St Augustine first worshipped.

HARBLEDOWN
St Nicholas:
179/130582
Originally the church of a leper hospital founded in 1084 by Lanfranc, builder of Canterbury cathedral. Norman and 13th C work in evidence.

HYTHE
St Leonard:
179/162349
Norman with later restoration, notably 13th and 14th C. Chancel contains finest Early English work in the county. 18th C tower. An unusual feature is the crypt and ambulatory stacked ceiling high with vast quantities of skulls and bones, all carefully separated and sized.

MINSTER-IN-SHEPPEY
St Mary & St Sexburga:
178/956730
Unusual in being two churches in one; N part originally serving nunnery founded in 670, S parochial and Early English.

Internally impressive and moving.

WROTHAM
St George:
188/612593
Sited actually on the old London Road, the tower has a vaulted passage beneath to allow public right of way to pass unhindered. Mainly 13th and 15th C; brasses; vaulted porch with room over.

Lancashire

LIVERPOOL CATHEDRAL
Church of Christ:
108/358903
Although often referred to as 'the last of the Gothic cathedrals', it is in fact modern in date, the foundation stone to this huge building perched on an imposing site, being laid in 1904 and the whole not completed until 1983.

By 1960 £2½ million had been spent on the building, all from public subscription and the generous gifts of Liverpool ship-owners.

Built of local sandstone, the cathedral designed by Sir Giles Gilbert Scott is 636ft in length, making it one of the greatest churches in any country. The work has twice been interrupted by war, and in World War II the S wall was damaged by a bomb and the Lady Chapel was put out of use until the late 1950s.

The central Vestry tower, 347ft in height, is one of the tallest structures of the world, and it shelters the heaviest peal of bells on earth. The cathedral also boasts the highest traverse arches of any church.

Internally, viewed from the W end of the nave, it is apparent that the great church was designed primarily as a preaching house rather than for the celebration of the liturgy.

LIVERPOOL, ROMAN CATHOLIC CATHEDRAL
Christ the King:
108/354894
Prompted by the sight of a new Anglican cathedral, it was decided in 1930 to commission Sir Edwin Lutyens to build a Roman Catholic cathedral on an even greater scale. From 1937 to 1940 work went on apace until shortage of money and the war brought the project to a halt; unfortunately, all this work has since disappeared.

On the cessation of hostilities, Cardinal Heenan, despairing of the amount of money needed to continue Lutyen's cathedral, launched a competition for the design of a new, cheaper building to fit the dawn of a new age – and to afford perfect visibility for a congregation of 2,000. The competition was won by Sir Frederick Gibberd.

From the first, both the design

and the materials were futuristic – steel and reinforced concrete – enclosing a circular space nearly 200ft across and illuminated by a colossal glazed lantern by Patrick Reyntiens to an idea of John Piper.

Sadly, this brave experiment has been criticized for failing to stand up to the rigours of time.

HALSALL
St Cuthbert:
108/370103
Architecturally an important church in the county. Of mainly 14th C date with a 15th C spire rising from a tower with an octagonal upper stage. There are spired turrets to each side of the chancel arch, one of which gave access to the rood-loft.

HEYSHAM
St Patrick's Chapel:
97/410617
Near to the ancient, though later parish church of St Peter. It was here the legendary St Patrick set up a monastery of which fragmentary ruins stand impressively over the cliff-top overlooking the sea. Notable doorway and a number of deep, shaped graves hollowed out of the solid rock with a hole at the head of each for the headstones, now lost.

SALMESBURY
St Leonard:
102/589304
Externally and internally of many periods, 16th C clerestoried nave, c1900 aisles and N tower. Norman font; Jacobean altar rails, 17th & 18th C lowered box pews and cut-down three-decker pulpit. There is evidence of old church customs: a funeral helm, sword and shield placed in the church after the death of the owner.

Leicestershire

LEICESTER CATHEDRAL
St Martin:
140/584051
The Church of St Martin was raised to cathedral status on the formation of the diocese in 1926. Predominantly 15th C in origin, it has been restored.

The tower, with broach spire, dates from 1867, replacing a Norman tower from the first church. The Vaughan Porch with muniments room above is another 19th C addition, and can be seen on the S side.

Inside, the 13th C nave has a hammer-beam roof of the last century with angels holding heraldic shields. The choir, too, was restored in the 19th C, but is a replica of its 15th C predecessor. The E window has good modern glass, and there is an attractive window dedicated to St Dunstan in the S chapel. The W bays are occupied by a military chapel and

the E by the chancellor's court – once the Lady Chapel, with grotesque corbels.

BREEDON-ON-THE-HILL
St Mary & St Hardulph:
129/406234
Sited within an Iron Age camp, the church was originally a Saxon monastery, and while today it is mainly Norman and 13th C, it is especially noted for a series of very fine 8th C carved stones.

GADDESBY
St Luke:
129/689131
A medievalist's delight (mainly from 1290 to 1340) its exterior, in particular the S aisle, is a riot of the 14th C stone-carver's art. Inside the church is graceful and light and noted for a life-size statue of Colonel Cheney on his horse at Waterloo.

LYDDINGTON
St Andrew:
141/877970
Predominantly Perpendicular which contains good wall-paintings; a sanctuary arranged in the 17th C manner, with the altar enclosed by railings on all four sides; brasses; and an unusual medieval accoustic jars in the chancel to help improve the quality of chanting, singing and preaching.

RYHALL
St John the Evangelist:
130/036108
St Tibba lived and died here c690. Against the W wall of the N aisle are the remains of a medieval hermitage associated with her, against which the first church was erected c1200.

STAUNTON HAROLD
Holy Trinity:
128/380209
Historically important church erected by Sir Robert Shirley in 1653, as a gesture of defiance against the Commonwealth, 'when', as an inscription over the door proclaims, 'all things sacred were throughout the nation either demolished or profaned'. For his actions Sir Robert was imprisoned in the Tower where he died in 1656. Today the church, externally Gothic but with a complete Jacobean interior, is cared for by the National Trust.

Lincolnshire

LINCOLN CATHEDRAL
Blessed Virgin Mary:
121/977718
Like Lichfield, this cathedral was originally established at nearby Stowe, which must have proved confusing and was probably the reason that the bishopric was transferred to Dorchester-on-Thames. After the Norman Conquest the see was presented to

Bishop Remigius for services, and it was he who settled the cathedra at Lincoln in a small Saxon Minster church.

This was rebuilt and consecrated in 1092. Fifty years later fire destroyed the wooden roof which was replaced with a stone vault. This and most of the church, was destroyed shortly after completion by an earthquake.

The famed St Hugh was elected to the bishopric the following year, 1186. He immediately set about raising money for its rebuilding which was completed 35 years after his death, in 1235. However, on his canonization in the same century, the E chevet which he had built was demolished and replaced with a new choir – the Angel Choir – which, with its square termination, is architecturally the cathedral's outstanding feature.

Externally, the W front is most noble and retains the deeply recessed doorways of the first building with the Gothic curtain wall of St Hugh. The remarkable panels depicting the sufferings of the damned are 12th C. The small turrets either side bear sculptures of St Hugh with his swan, and the swineherd of Stowe who gave his life's savings to the building.

The central tower of the Norman building collapsed in 1237 and was replaced by the present splendid one in the following century.

Internally, the immense nave was erected in 1235, but the W termination retains a portion of the earlier church.

The choir was completed prior to the nave in the late 12th C. The stalls are 13th C and have no less than 100 original misericords of the total of 700 remaining in all British cathedrals. Unfortunately, Wren's reredos to the high altar is not in keeping.

Beyond the altar is the Angel Choir (1260–80) with the famous Lincoln Imp high on the N wall and the place of Hugh's burial marked by the paving. Of the rich shrine there are no remains.

BARLINGS
St Edward, King & Martyr:
121/076749
Originally Norman, the church was built near the ruins of a Premonstratensian monastery whose abbot was hanged for his part in the Lincolnshire Rising of 1536.

LITTLE BYTHAM
St Medard:
130/013181
An ancient, pleasing church with Saxon work and an interesting early tympanum over the S door which once possibly contained the skull and arm bone of St Medard, the patron saint.

MARKBY
St Peter:
122/487790
Externally, with its thatched roof, it reminds us of how the great majority of England's humble

parish churches might have looked. Inside, 17th C with box pews and two-decker pulpit.

PINCHBECK
St Mary:
131/242256
A restored church of the Decorated and Perpendicular periods. Of interest is the early 19th C graveside shelter for the protection of the vicar in inclement weather.

RAITHBY
Chapel (Methodist):
122/3767
Typical of early non-conformist places of worship, it was adapted from a stable in the corner of a stable yard to the hall and bears the inscription 'Wesley's Chapel Built by Robert Carr Brackenbury 1779, Dedicated July 5 1779 by John Wesley'. Internally, quite simple. From the vestibule a divided stair (men right, women left) leads to a landing and gallery.

London,
City and Greater

LONDON, ST PAUL'S CATHEDRAL
The distinctive dome of St Paul's caps the second great cathedral on the present site, and through the former Old St Paul's it occupies one of the most ancient Christian sites in England.

The first church was destroyed by fire in 675, its successor was sacked by Viking pirates, and the building of the Norman church was itself interrupted by fire. Consequently, the completion of Old St Paul's did not occur until 1315. In 1447 the spire, the highest in Europe at that time, was struck by lightning, and in the 16th C the cloisters were demolished for their stone. The restoration of the building, begun in 1632, ceased with the Civil War, and Cromwell in fact used the church as a barracks.

Following the Great Fire of London in 1666, Christopher Wren was commissioned to restore the cathedral. After removing 47,000 cart-loads of rubbish, he commenced to build anew. The erection of the present St Paul's was not without incident, and the design of today bears little resemblance to the first agreed plans.

The W front dominates the approach from Ludgate Hill, with double portico and pillared towers flanking the Grecian columns.

The splendid dome, topped by a glittering cross, is formed of a stone cone covered by an outer dome of wood with a skin of lead.

Internally, from the W end there is an uninterrupted view to the high altar following the removal of the organ screen in the 19th C, the loss of which also allows visitors to

experience the magnificent view of the dome's interior, with its beautiful 18th C frescoes.

By contrast, the crypt, the largest in Europe, is quite dismal. It is only relieved by the handsome Chapel of the Order of the British Empire at its E end. Nelson is buried here in a 16th C sarcophagus intended for Cardinal Wolsey. But the most touching memorial is the plain grave of Wren himself, inscribed: 'Si monumentum requiris, circumspice' – 'If you seek his monument, look around you.'

SOUTHWARK CATHEDRAL
St Saviour & St Mary Overie
The site was occupied by a monastery in the reign of Edward the Confessor, but in 1106 a new church was built which was re-dedicated 70 years later to Thomas à Becket following his murder at Canterbury. Fire destroyed this building in 1212 and rebuilding was begun in the middle of the same century, but not completed until 1310. Fire again damaged the church in 1385 and the 15th C saw further restoration, including the heightening of the central tower.

At the dissolution of the monasteries it became a parish church and in 1614 was purchased by the parishioners. In the 18th C it fell into disrepair, two of its chapels were demolished, and in the following century the nave was left roofless. Barely saved from demolition, the church received a new nave in 1890 and was adopted as the cathedral of a diocese formed in 1905.

Inside, there is considerable medieval work as one would expect in a cathedral of such antiquity and prominence. The building has many associations with the famous, in particular Edmund, the younger brother of William Shakespeare, who is buried in the church. A N transept chapel is in memory of John Harvard who, in 1638, emigrated to America and founded there the university which bears his name.

WESTMINSTER ABBEY
St Peter
Historically, the church was founded as an early Saxon monastery in the 7th C, but was later destroyed by the Danes. It was refounded by St Dunstan c960 as a priory in the charge of Benedictine monks, which subsequently grew to be the richest abbey in Britain, predominantly due to its royal patronage. It was dissolved in 1540 by Henry VIII, but re-established in 1556 only to be dissolved again in 1559.

Architecturally, the church and substantial monastic remains are of a considerable number of periods dating from the church of Edward the Confessor (c1065); the Lady Chapel (early 13th C); the nave (14th and 15th C); W window and nave roof (late 15th C). But of particular note is undoubtedly Henry VII's Chapel

with its magnificent pendant-vaulted roof, the highest achievement of English ecclesiastical architecture, which was built between 1503 and c1512 and restored in the early 19th C.

Once described as 'the jewel in the Empire's crown', the church is the repository of the major memorials of British national figures, and is the stage for most state religious occasions.

WESTMINSTER, ROMAN CATHOLIC CATHEDRAL
Church of the Most Precious Blood
One of the major Catholic churches in the country, both spiritually and architecturally. Designed by J.F. Bentley, it was commenced at the close of the 19th C when the winds of change were blowing through the cloisters of church architectural thinking. This is reflected in Bentley's brief to produce a church in an Italian or Byzantine style, rather than in the more traditional Gothic.

Undoubtedly this is a building of visual note, mostly because Bentley favoured a polychromatic effect of alternating layers of contrasting red brick and white stone. Now that the clutter to the W end has been cleared away, this effect is further heightened by the red-and-white piazza pavement, which creates a truly sensational architectural panorama.

The building consists of four linked domes, the nave taking up the first three and the chancel the fourth. The whole building is dominated by a 284ft campanile tower to the N of the W front. This latter is itself a spectacular feature composed of a giant Italianate porch with a series of domed pinnacles, diminishing in size as they recess and ascend.

Internally, however, the church has suffered in that the sumptuous richness that was envisaged was not completed. Only in the Lady Chapel has Bentley's scheme been finished, and one can admire the marble and mosaics which should have covered the whole cathedral inside.

GREENWICH
St Luke
This 17th C brick country church survives in a charming old churchyard near to Charlton House. Inside unspoilt, it has some contemporary monuments and glass, and fine hatchments of differing dates.

GRESHAM STREET
St Anne & St Agnes, Aldersgate
Built by Wren 1677–80, the tower was added in 1714. It was gutted in 1940 and subsequently restored and reopened in 1966, and is now used by the Lutherans. Externally inconspicuous, the interior is a complete contrast – magnificent plaster-vault ceilings, brilliant colour, and woodwork of the highest quality, some of which is the original. The best is the elegant

altar-piece.

NEWHAM
St Mary Magdalene
A complete 12th C church near to the docks of East London. Fine interlace arcading along the chancel wall; Norman apse with excellent monument to Edward Neville, Earl of Westmorland and his wife; wall-paintings; elegant marble font dated 1639.

ST MARY-AT-HILL
St Mary-at-Hill
By Wren 1670–76, the plain exterior gives no indication of the riches within – sumptuous interior, rich and bold plaster-work, fine fittings. But its greatest glory must be the wood- and iron-work. The iron sword-rests of various Georgian dates are the best in London.

STEPNEY
St Dunstan
A large church set in a village-like churchyard full of monuments to Georgian sailors. Architecturally it is late medieval with ancient origins. Inside is a rare Saxon rood of stone over the high altar.

UPPER THAMES STREET
St Bennet, Paul's Wharfe
Wren church 1677–83. Of red brick with contrasting stone dressings and swags above the windows. The tower is capped with a lead dome and lantern, the roofs, however, retain the old tiles. The interior is one of the least altered in the City, containing galleries, wainscoted walls, W organ and carved Renaissance altar-piece.

WEST SMITHFIELD
St Bartholomew-the-Great
An imposing Norman building which is only the partial remains (choir and transepts) of a much larger monastic church. The main W gate-house survives, together with a single side of the cloister. The 17th C brick tower contains the oldest ring of bells in England. Inside, vast and dark in the mystic Romanesque manner. Of note, a Perpendicular watching window.

Manchester, Greater

MANCHESTER CATHEDRAL
St Mary, St Denys & St George:
109/838986
Although the bishopric dates only from 1847, the site of the cathedral is an ancient one, originating in all probability from that of a Saxon church. The present building, however, enters history in 1398 when a priest inherited a local manor, made it into a community house for eight others and was granted a charter allowing him to erect a church. But the existing building has seen drastic restoration and little of the 14th C

fabric remains.
    The W tower was rebuilt in 1867, when the original was in ruins, but the internal arch is a relic of the 14th C. Both N and S porches are 19th C.
    Inside, most of the fabric and fittings are of 15th C date, overlaid with Victorian restoration which has been closely modelled on the old, and is quite successful.
    The clerestory windows of the nave were added at the close of the 15th C, and in the same century the windows of the nave aisles were removed to allow the construction of additional aisles N and S for the provision of chantry chapels. Until the 19th C the wooden screens dividing these chapels were in situ and their removal has made the church one of the widest in the country. The choir is also 15th C work. There are many other features of interest.

ASHTON-UNDER-LYNE
St Michael:
109/931989
An unfortunate setting, and in common with numerous churches in the area, it has suffered under Victorian zeal. But despite this, the church retains an important collection of stained glass c1500: in particular, 18 scenes from the Life of St Helena, and the figures of kings.

MANCHESTER
St Anne:
109/837984
A fine and gracious town church, providing an oasis of tranquility in an otherwise commercial city. Erected in 1709–12, in the style of Wren, of red sandstone which has mellowed well. Internally, Classical, galleried and arcaded with a flat coved ceiling and good carved frieze in the E apse. Much contemporary woodwork.

WARBURTON
St Werburgh:
109/697896
This church is more typical of adjoining Cheshire, insomuch as it is of timber, with some walls replaced with stone (1645), and brick (1711) – the date of the brick tower. Inside, constructional timbers divide off the aisles. Most of the fittings are Jacobean. The box pews are 19th C.

Norfolk

NORWICH CATHEDRAL
Holy & Undivided Trinity:
134/235089
Historically, the siting of Norwich is the result of a chequered history. It was originally formed from the Saxon see of East Anglia, with its cathedral – probably of wood – at Dunwich. Later the see was divided and a cathedral built at North Elmham in 673, the wooden

building being replaced by one of stone in the following century. This was destroyed by the Danes in 870 and left in ruins until rebuilt in 950. However, with the arrival of the Normans, the see was moved to the more populated centre of Thetford, and later to Norwich, where the present church was erected in 1095.
    Externally, the most noticeable feature is the series of flying buttresses supporting the clerestory of the choir, a 14th C addition which makes an impressive sight.
    The W door is early 15th C and the window above was inserted in 1470. The tower is 12th C, the lower stage being completed prior to 1119. The original spire was blown down in a gale in 1362, and its successor struck by lightning almost exactly a century later. Consequently, the present spire is 15th C.
    Three of the monastic gateways survive: the Erpingham Gate (1420), the Ethelbert Gate and the Water Gate adjacent to the river.
    Internally, the earliest part of the fabric is the nave, erected before 1145 but with the lierne vault added in the same year as the W window. Both transepts are 12th C, and have 16th C vaults. Of particular note are the roof bosses.
    The choir stalls date back to 1420 and have fine misericords, and there is a 14th C lectern. The presbytery is unique in retaining its apsidal termination. The clerestory and vault were damaged by the fall of the spire in 1362 and the present lierne vault was built by Bishop Goldwell at the end of the 15th C, the actual clerestory windows having been restored by his predecessor.
    The ancient episcopal throne, raised on steps behind the altar, is the most precious possession of the cathedral and incorporates Saxon stones of the original church situated at Dunwich. This is the only English cathedral having its cathedra positioned E of the altar.
    Of the original monastic buildings, only the ruins of the refectory and doorways which once led to various domestic rooms remain. The cloisters are a rebuild following destruction by rioters between 1297 and 1430, and they are perhaps the finest work of its type in the country. Benches scratched with the play-boards of novices' games are of especial charm.

ATTLEBOROUGH
St Mary:
144/048954
A magnificent church sadly engulfed by the 20th C. Norman chancel and 14th C nave. The chancel was collegiate at one time, the nave being erected for parochial use later. Unrivalled anywhere in E Anglia is the rood screen with intact rood loft, which stretches right across from N to S, and is topped by frescoes c1500, all the more remarkable for its colour and liveliness after all these

centuries.

BEESTON REGIS
All Saints:
133/174432
Here, in this cliff-top church, in a county famed for the quality of its painted panels, those on the beautiful 15th C rood screen surpass all.

BRISLEY
St Bartholomew:
132/951215
Predominantly Perpendicular architecture with a striking W tower. Inside, three-decker pulpit; 15th C screen; and good font cover. An interesting feature is the crypt situated beneath the altar, supposed to have been used to lodge prisoners on their way to Norwich gaol.

BURNHAM THORPE
All Saints:
132/853418
Lord Nelson's father was rector here, and the interior is resplendent with many memorials to Nelson himself, as well as relics of the Admiral.

EAST DEREHAM
St Nicholas:
132/989134
Historically and architecturally interesting church with work of many periods and styles. Norman S doorway; early 16th C detached tower; Decorated nave, transepts and chancel with fine sedilia, piscina and aumbry niche for the storage of the communion vessels. In the churchyard is the well of St Withburga, daughter of King Annas, who founded a convent here.

GT YARMOUTH
St Nicholas:
134/530073
This is the largest parish church in England and it does not disappoint the ardent church-crawler. Begun in the 12th C each successive generation extended the building. Unfortunately, it was all destroyed in 1942. Many of the old fittings are therefore from other churches, but they are well arranged to create an impressive church.

HALES
St Margaret:
134/384962
A text-book church, typical of the county. Round tower, apse, fine Norman doorways and a charming thatched roof. Inside, wall-paintings and screen. Sadly, its isolation has meant redundancy, and it is now vested in the RCF.

HEACHAM
St Mary:
132/682380
Particularly noted for its monuments, especially one to Pocahontas, Red Indian wife of John Rolfe, who was squire of the manor in the reign of James I.

NORWICH
Octagonal Chapel (Unitarian):
134/2308
Undoubtedly the finest of all non-conformist places of worship. An elegant mid-18th C brick building of architectural complexity designed by Thomas Ivory, a provincial carpenter. Detail is restrained and all the more effective for it. Instead it relies on form to achieve a sense of richness. Illumination is via a dome supported on massive Corinthian columns carried from floor level through the gallery front, and which are then linked to each other by a series of arches, quite stunning.

SPARHAM
St Mary:
133/071197
A noble exterior, mainly Perpendicular, with an exceptionally tall tower. Scratched onto a door jamb is a mass clock, similar to a sundial, but which served to tell the times of the church services. This was obviously done before the building was completed. Inside are panels of the old screen, brasses, bench-ends and a good roof.

TIVETSHALL
St Margaret:
156/164871
Contains a rare treasure which is possibly the finest of its type in existence – the Royal Arms of Elizabeth I in the tympanum above the chancel arch.

TRUNCH
St Botolph:
133/286348
A medievalist's delight, full of interest and history. Of particular note are a screen of 1502; medieval glass; a fine 15th C roof with angels; return stalls with holes for ink pots and much graffiti, evidence that a school was once held here; and the greatest glory, an almost unique wooden font-cover c1500 over a font of 1390.

UPPER SHERINGHAM
All Saints:
133/145418
Famous for its 15th C rood screen with loft; a painted beam with pulley for raising the ornate font cover; and excellent bench-ends with quaint scenes including a mermaid, a nurse with Christ child, and a cat with kitten.

WALPOLE
St Peter:
131/503168
Even in its reduced circumstances, perhaps the finest church in the county, both inside and out. Unusual is the processional way under the E end. Vast Perpendicular windows; fine porches, especially two-storey S, and numerous other interesting features.

WESTOW LONGUEVILLE
All Saints:
133/114158
James Woodforde, who wrote the *Diary of a Country Parson*, was rector here 1776–1803. His portrait and memorial are in the church. Other notable features include the sedilia and piscina, for pouring away consecrated wine after communion, and the S aisle window with figures of the Apostles.

WYMONDHAM
St Mary & St Thomas of Canterbury:
144/106015
An important and noble church with twin towers E and W. Originally part of a Benedictine abbey, it was also always parochial. Predominantly Norman, with splendid arcades and triforium, while above is a clerestory and magnificent roof of 15th C date. Nice two-storey in which can be seen the famous Corporas Case, a rare example of a 13th C Opus Anglicanum.

Northamptonshire

PETERBOROUGH CATHEDRAL
St Peter, St Paul & St Andrew:
142/195986
The first abbey is reputed to have been planned by Peada, king of Mercia in the 7th C, but he was assassinated before he could begin the work. Later his brother Wulfhere, who had slain his two sons for adopting the Christian faith, was brought to repentance by St Chad and ordered to build the abbey as his penance. On its completion it was dedicated to St Peter and the town, previously known as Medeshamsted, was renamed Peterborough.

In 870 the church was burned down by the Danes and the monks murdered. For 100 years it remained in ruins until rebuilt in 972 by Aethelwold, Bishop of Winchester, in obedience to a vision. The following century it was burned down by Hereward the Wake in protest at the appointment of a Norman abbot, and finally rebuilt, largely in its present form, in 1192. On its surrender at the dissolution it was made a cathedral, the last abbot becoming the first bishop.

Much damage was done to the fabric and furnishings by Cromwell's armies, and it was not until the 19th C that it was fully restored.

The W front, possibly the most splendid example of late Romanesque architecture in the country, was built in 1237, with flanking towers to act as buttresses. At the close of the 14th C a porchway was added to the central arch. The W doors are of medieval wood.

The magnificent Romanesque nave was built in 1220 and retains its original wooden vault, the colouring restored. The Perpendicular windows in the nave aisles, however, were inserted in the 15th C.

Either side of the W doors are mural paintings executed at the end of the 16th C and depicting the sexton who buried both Katherine of Aragon and Mary, Queen of Scots. Both queens had graves in the cathedral, but Mary's was moved to London by her son.

The choir's ceiling is richly ornamented. The stalls are 19th C with carvings either side depicting the vision of Aethelwold and the story of King Oswald. The windows of the apse behind the high altar have 14th C tracery and some medieval glass.

The E extension was added shortly before the dissolution, early in the 16th C.

ASHBY ST LEGER
St Leodegorius:
152/576832
A rare dedication of a saint who gave his name to the village and, ultimately, a horse race. Associated with the Catesby family, once of a nearby hall, where the gunpowder conspirators met. There is a brass of William Catesby, beheaded after the battle of Bosworth, in the church. Numerous features include beautiful rood screen, benches and musicians' pew.

BRIXWORTH
All Saints:
141/748713
Probably the most important early Saxon building in the county, with extensive 7th C work in evidence and later 10th C, it is truly a period showpiece. Roman tiles are used a great deal internally. The church was monastic, which explains its size and numerous liturgical components. These include the narthex at W end and apse at E. Slight remodelling in the Middle Ages and 19th C.

CHARWELTON
Holy Trinity:
151/545555
A relic of changing fortunes, now isolated when the nearby road was diverted following the War of Roses. Architectural features include fine priest's room over S porch.

FINEDON
St Mary:
141/913719
A stately, Decorated period edifice chiefly remembered for the excellent private theological library over the S porch.

STANFORD-ON-AVON
St Nicholas:
140/588788
Light and airy, this church is most famous for its 17th C organ-case, expelled by Cromwell from Whitehall, than for any other feature. However, there is a splendid E window with 14th–

16th C stained glass. Archbishop Laud was once rector here.

SULGRAVE
St James:
152/556454
Traditional English church, not too large, not too small. Important historical association with the USA: the Washington family were lords of the manor here from 1540 until 1659. Brass to Lawrence Washington of Sulgrave manor 1584. Small panel of stained glass depicts earliest representation of Washington arms.

Northumberland

ANCROFT
St Anne:
75/003452
A Norman foundation with, at the W end, a 14th C 'Vicars Pele' or fortified tower: a relic of the county's troubled past when it was often ravaged by Scottish raiders.

HEXHAM
St Andrew:
87/935642
The first church was built here by Wilfrid c675, and of this the crypt alone remains, though some of the passages are closed, and a display of church treasures has been incorporated which mars the atmosphere. In 876 this church was laid waste by the Danes and not refounded until 1113, and then as an Augustinian priory. Among the many splendid and varied medieval features, of particular note are the unique monks' night stairs remaining from the priory, and a Saxon 'Frith' stool.

HOLY ISLAND
St Mary the Virgin:
75/125418
A 13th C church completed in the 18th C. It stands adjacent to the ruins of one of England's most hallowed spots, the monastery founded by St Aidan in 635 at the invitation of King Oswald. This was destroyed in 875 by marauding Danes.

Nottinghamshire

SOUTHWELL CATHEDRAL
Blessed Virgin Mary:
120/703537
Often incorrectly styled Southwell Minster, it is a collegiate church of great antiquity and it was justly natural that it should become the cathedral of diocese newly formed in 1884.

Founded in the 7th C by St Paulinus it occupies a Roman site, possibly a basilica, and a tessalated pavement from this survives in the

S transept. Around 1109 a new Norman church was begun, but this only existed in its entirety for a century. In c1230 Archbishop Gray, who was responsible for the great transepts of York and the W front of Ripon, commenced on extensions and rebuilding work.

Architecturally, Southwell embodies evidence of many styles and periods. The W and central towers are 12th C; the W door is Romanesque; the doorway of the N transept has a Saxon tympanum. The vestibule and Chapter House were built at the close of the 13th C; the choir is early 14th C as is the screen dividing the nave from choir, which is probably the greatest treasure of Southwell and has no rival in the country. It is particularly noted for its 300 sculptured heads and figures from biblical stories, English and church history.

HAWTON
All Saints:
120/788512
Externally, mainly 15th C surmounted by a fine tower. The E window is curvilinear and exhibits superb 14th C stonework. Internally simple with old pews. The Easter Sepulchre is the finest in the county, and there are well-executed sedilia, which bear a striking resemblance to craftsmanship seen at Southwell.

NEWARK
St Mary Magdalene:
120/799539
A town church in the grand manner with transepts, aisles, nave and choir under the shadow of a splendid spire. Inside there is a great deal of 15th C woodwork including poppy-heads and screen and a number of modern additions, with a 1937 Comper reredos and sculptural contributions from R. Kiddey.

Oxfordshire

OXFORD CATHEDRAL
Church of Christ:
164/516060
The first church was erected here in 730 by Didanus, a local king, in memory of his wife. He later founded a nunnery for his daughter which was rebuilt in 1122, and it was from these, the church and the nunnery, that the present cathedral grew. At the dissolution, Henry VIII presented church and endowments to his favourite, Wolsey, who proceeded to demolish the cloisters and W bays of the nave to obtain stone for the building of Christ Church college. The total destruction of the church was prevented only by his fall from grace. The church now fulfills the dual role of cathedral and college chapel.

The most notable architectural feature of the church is the 13th C

spire, which is reputed to be the oldest in the country.

Internally, the church is unique in retaining five Norman vaults, including that of the sacristy. The timbered roof of the nave is 16th C and that of the lantern 17th. The 12th C nave arcades are of rare design, but the N nave aisle is 15th C.

Behind the choir stalls are finely wrought iron screens. The base of St Frideswide's shrine, made in 1289 and displaying the earliest known leaf sculpture, stands in the N choir aisle. Nearby is the 15th C wooden watching chamber, one of only two remaining examples, with chantry chapel beneath.

ABINGDON
Ock Street Chapel (Baptist):
164/4997
A particularly good example of a severe Classical style chapel, nicely situated within its own graveyard.

BURFORD
St John the Baptist:
163/254124
The epitomy of an English village and an English church. Internally the effect is largely 15th C, and it was the treatment of this which impelled William Morris to start the 'Antiscrape' movement as a reaction to Victorian over-restoration.

COTE Near BAMPTON
(Baptist):
164/351031
Built in 1664, it retains a charming, untouched interior with gallery, flag-stone floor, box pews, communion table, and possibly the earliest surviving baptistry within a chapel.

IFFLEY
St Mary the Virgin:
164/526035
A text-book church of late Norman work, rich with detail of the period. Beakhead and zig-zag carving. Pleasantly dark and mysterious.

KELMSCOTT
St George:
163/249994
Historical association with William Morris, artist, writer, social reformer, whose tomb is in the churchyard.

RYCOTE
St Michael & All Angels:
165/666047
Now in the custody of the DoE. Queen Elizabeth I and Charles I worshipped here in this remote, parkland chapel to nearby house. Sumptuous interior full of diverse fittings.

Shropshire

BATTLEFIELD
St Mary Magdalene:
126/528043
Founded in 1406 as a chantry chapel to commemorate the dead of the battle of Shrewsbury in 1403. Predominantly 15th C with later reticulated tracery to some windows. Unfortunately, by the 19th C the nave had lost its roof and become ruinous, but was restored in 1861–62.

ONIBURY
St Michael:
137/455792
A rural simplicity, which echoes the crafts of our forefathers, is captured in this Norman church of tower, nave and chancel. Plenty of rough-hewn oak in the W gallery, pews, and the old guileless roof. A Decalogue, or panel of Ten Commandments, dates from 1902.

STOKESAY
St John:
137/436817
The consequence of siting a church next to a castle can be seen here – during the Civil War, this church was much damaged, and subsequently had to be rebuilt and refurnished, the nave in 1654, the tower in 1664.

TONG
St Mary the Virgin with St Bartholomew:
127/795074
Victorian restoration has left its scars on this large and grand church of 1410, but nevertheless the monuments are some of the best and most important in England. The 'Golden Chapel' erected as a chantry just over 100 years after the foundation of the church is notable, retaining its old stencilled walls, its gilt fan-vaulted ceiling, and beautiful effigies.

Somerset

WELLS CATHEDRAL
St Andrew:
182/553458
The diocese was founded in 909, and a first church was built about that time. But with the coming of the Normans began two centuries of troubled history.

In 1088 the buildings were allowed to become ruinous when Bishop de Villula removed the see to Bath. A compromise was attempted in 1136, when Bath and Wells were united, both churches housing the cathedra of the bishop, but this survived only until 1192 when Bishop Savaric assumed the title of Bishop of Bath & Glastonbury. His successor retained only the title of Bishop of Bath. Finally the pope decreed in 1244 that the see should be that of

Bath and Wells, and this title has been used ever since, although the cathedra belongs to Wells exclusively.

New buildings were erected in 1148 and 1184, and the fabric was damaged by an earthquake in 1248.

The W front, dating from 1239, is among the most magnificent architectural achievements of the 13th C. The same can be said of its restoration in modern times. Today, its statues, once brilliantly coloured and backed by gilded niches, will survive for many more centuries.

The central tower was built in the 12th C as far as the stringcourse and its upper portion added in 1321. The SW tower dates from 1386, the NW from 1424.

Internally, the church derives a unity of form from the almost complete building of 1186. The most striking features are the great scissor arches, erected in 1360 to receive the weight of the heightened tower. Also of the same date, and second only in fame, is the beautiful 'heavenly stairway' which gives access to the fine Chapter House on the N side.

Unique to Wells are the medieval houses, chapel and dining room once provided for the vicars-choral, which no other cathedral has retained.

BABINGTON
St Margaret:
183/669507
Unequivocally Georgian, this church is complete and unaltered, making it the most splendid example of its type in the county. Interestingly, it has an apsidal sanctuary, and the W tower, though small, is topped with a cupola.

BRYMPTON D'EVERCY
St Andrew:
183/518154
Part of a group; manor house, outbuildings and charnel house. Predominantly 14th–15th C with an ornate bell-cote instead of tower or spire. Inside is a fine stone screen of early 15th C date.

CULBONE
St Culbone:
181/843483
Of Norman origin, the building is arguably the smallest parish church in England, but still manages to contain a 17th C screen, old benches, and a family pew. Externally it carries a quaint diminutive spire.

LULLINGTON
All Saints:
183/784519
A Norman church with original tripartite plan rich in period detail notably the N door with Christ in Majesty, and inside a massive font inscribed 'In this holy font sins perish and are washed away'.

111

TRULL
All Saints:
193/216223
Perpendicular, inside is a treasure house of late medieval art: rood-screen, pulpit with painted panels depicting the Doctors, a fine array of carved bench-ends and an unusually extensive series of late 15th C glass.

WATCHET
Chapel (Baptist):
181/064426
A chapel of unusual architectural quality, owing its outward appearance to Spanish influences in the gentle, ogee-curved gable end. Dated 1824, architectural lettering across the front is particularly good.

WITHAM
St Mary, St John Baptist & All Saints:
183/734412
A small, late 12th C 'French' church, apsidal and stone-vaulted, which was possibly erected by Sir Hugh, later Bishop of Lincoln, who came from Burgundy as prior of the first English Carthusian monastery, founded here by Henry II.

Staffordshire

LICHFIELD CATHEDRAL
Blessed Virgin Mary & St Chad:
128/115097
Today's cathedral site replaces an earlier one established by Bishop Chad c669 across the pool adjacent to the present church, at Stowe, which was then moved when a cathedral was founded to receive the shrine of Bishop Chad in 700. Briefly, in 786, the see was raised to an archbishopric, but 17 years later it was merged with Chester and Coventry, and only in the last century was the present diocese formed.

A new church was built for the saint's shrine in the 12th C. The building suffered appalling damage at the hands of the Cromwellians who seized the Close in 1643; 2,000 cannon shots and 1,500 grenades are said to have been fired against the fabric, the central tower battered down and the church left roofless and in ruins. Subsequent restoration, notably by Wyatt and G.G. Scott, have produced a somewhat banal building whose best impression is gained from a distance.

Despite the vicissitudes visited upon it, this is the only English cathedral to retain its three spires, the W pair being completed in 1320 and the central a 17th C rebuild of the one demolished by Roundhead bombardment.

The W front is an ill-conceived restoration of the original built in 1293, and only five of the 'king' statues are of that date, the remainder being unworthy

Victorian reproductions.

Internally, the nave was erected in 1258, completing the rebuilding of the Norman cathedral of the 12th C.

The choir, standing at the same level as the nave, but at a noticeable angle to it, was the earliest part of the present church to be constructed some time at the close of the 12th C. The deflection of choir and nave was most probably dictated by the site, and not as often asserted, as a symbolic representation of the crucifixion; the cruciform church has no significance.

The Chapter House, with central column and canopied stalls, was erected in 1249 and is approached through a cloister-like vestibule. This was the only part of the cathedral to retain its roof after the Civil War ravages.

BRADLEY
All Saints:
127/880180
Of great antiquarian interest is this 13th–15th C church, with its well-lit nave containing well-proportioned arcades of c1260. It has a carved Norman tub font, and a medieval rood-stair leading to a modern rood screen; a little good glass and 16th C effigies.

ECCLESHALL
Holy Trinity:
127/828292
Here can be seen the tombs of four bishops of Lichfield, of which the 17th C memorial to Bishop Overton is the finest of all. Two other features of interest are the mass clock, similiar to a sundial but which indicates the times of the church services, and a relic of an old church custom, arrow whets on the S side, made by those practising archery in the churchyard after service – a fineable offence if not undertaken.

TAMWORTH
St Editha:
139/208042
The church is generally of noble and ample proportion and mostly 14th C although there is Norman and 15th C work in evidence, and 17th–18th C fittings. But the most notable aspect is the unique double staircase in the W tower.

Suffolk

BURY ST EDMUNDS CATHEDRAL
St James:
155/856640
From the 7th C a church has existed at Bury – or Beodricsworth as it was called. But in 903, the body of Edmund, king of East Anglia, brutally murdered for not denying his faith, was buried here in a wooden church and forever afterwards, in remembrance, the town has been known as Bury St

Edmund. Since then a number of churches have occupied the site. In 1032 a new church was erected and the secular clergy in custody of the shrine of St Edmund were replaced by monks. In 1095 a further church was constructed, and subsequently the attached monastery was soon one of the wealthiest and most famed in Christendom.

In 1214, the abbey church was the stage for the signing of the Magna Carta between the English barons and King John.

The present cathedral is a further rebuild commenced in 1438, but not completed until the reign of Edward VI, with extensive additions taking place during the present century.

Architecturally, the church is dominated by the bell-tower erected in the 12th C as the principal entrance to the abbey. But of the medieval periods, only the nave of 1438 survives, although some remains of the third church of 1095 can be seen in the churchyard, and fragments of masonry from the 12th C church are built into the N wall.

Internally the church is predominantly modern.

ALDEBURGH
St Peter & St Paul:
156/464568
Immortalized in George Crabbe's book, *The Borough*, this church achieved its present symmetrical plan with broad aisles in the late 16th C. A likeness of the Reverend author by Thurlow of nearby Saxmundham, can be seen in the N aisle.

AMPTON
St Peter:
155/866713
Here, the most notable features are the chantry chapel of 1479, and the church's greatest treasure, a 'sealed Book' of Common Prayer – neither the British Museum nor the Bodleian Library possess a copy.

BLYTHBURGH
Holy Trinity:
156/451754
A huge 15th C edifice, though much reduced in beauty by the 17th C iconoclast William Dowsing, it was founded on the wealth of the town when it was a port of some repute. Magnificent contemporary woodwork including tie-beam roof, carved bench-ends and carved chancel stalls, some of which are obviously fronted by the removed rood-loft.

BRAMFIELD
St Andrew:
156/398737
A tiny village church with thatched roof and very early detached circular tower. Internally, the beautiful screen with vaulting is the best of its type in the county. Also here is the most important piece of Renaissance art in England,

Nicholas Stone's exquisite effigy of 1634.

CAVENDISH
St Mary:
155/805466
The epitomy of an English village and English church, whose clerestory exterior is decorated with flint flushwork in panels similar to Long Melford. 14th C tower with the curious feature of a ringing-chamber furnished as a living-room complete with fireplace and original window shutters. Two fine medieval lecterns, one 15th C brass the other 16th C wood.

COMBS
St Mary:
155/051569
Architecturally, Decorated and Perpendicular periods, containing in the S aisle windows a series of magnificent 15th C stained glass panels depicting the Old Testament kings and prophets and the genealogy of Christ; the Works of Mercy; the Tree of Jesse, and most impressive of all, scenes from the life of St Margaret of Antioch. The whole reminds us that the medieval church was not the drab shell we know it today, but rather a riot of vivid colour and pattern designed to illuminate the lives of a population who were mostly uneducated and needed the Bible stories graphically illustrated.

DENINGTON
St Mary:
156/282670
A magnificent church chiefly remarkable for its aisle and parclose screens, complete with lofts and parapets. Much 15th C work predominates with other 17th and 18th C fittings. A great rarity is the cover for the pyx (vessel in which the host is preserved and suspended in front of the altar).

ICKLINGHAM
All Saints:
155/770730
Now in the care of the RCF, this church has seen a great deal of destruction by Reformers and Puritans, but there still remains considerable work by medieval craftsmen. Superb parish chest in which the church's documents would have been kept, and of historical interest are the original kneelers cut from thick tufts of reeds from which the word 'hassock' is derived.

IPSWICH
Friar Street Chapel (Unitarian):
169/1644
Originally built as a Presbyterian chapel c1700 for a cost of £257 by Joseph Clarke, carpenter, it was visited by Daniel Defoe in 1722 who wrote of it 'as large and as fine a building of that kind as most on this side of England'. The furnishings inside command attention and include a beautiful wine-glass pulpit thought to be by Grindling Gibbons and a gallery

clock with painted face showing both roman and arabic numerals which predates the building. Some of the box pews have hinged flaps for book rests.

KEDINGTON
St Peter & St Paul:
154/705470
Predominantly Perpendicular, but with earlier work including the chancel, this is one of the finest of the Puritan churches. A striking 16th C hammer-beam roof overlooks much excellent 17th and 18th C woodwork, which sets the atmosphere of the inside. Of great interest is the vault in which there are over 50 lead coffins, some of them moulded to the exact shape of the body.

SHELLAND
King Charles the Martyr:
155/017604
Ecclesiastically unusual, this parish is 'donative', meaning that it was the personal possession of the patron – which probably accounts for the unusual dedication. With box pews and a three-decker pulpit of fine proportions, this small church was one of the most attractive 18th C interiors in the county.

WALPOLE
Chapel (Congregational):
156/365745
Considered to have been converted from two cottages, this thatched-roof village non-conformist place of worship is the second oldest Congregational chapel in England, and is still in use. Architecturally, it gave rise to the Congregational Meeting Houses of New England, USA. The interior remains totally unaltered, and in its peaceful graveyard setting with stately headstones, it is a delight to visit.

Surrey

GUILDFORD CATHEDRAL
Holy Spirit:
186/985500
A modern cathedral both in time and style of architecture. The bishopric was created in 1927 and the foundation stone of Sir Edward Maufe's cathedral was laid in 1936. Completion was delayed by the war years, and so it was not until 1961 that it was ready for dedication.
Fashioned of bricks made from local clay, its uncompromising presence dominates the city from an imposing site on the hill above. A stark monument, the interior could be described as severe. Certainly the exterior is spartan, enlivened only by a fine Eric Gill sculpture on the E end and sculptured figures above the buttresses.
Inside one is conscious of its great width and height, and on a

sunny day, the quality of light streaming through the clear glass. But there is also modern stained glass of interesting design to be seen.

COMPTON
St Nicholas:
186/954471
Set within a magnificent unspoilt graveyard of ancient date, though under threat, this church is of 11th C origin. Here, the only two-storeyed sanctuary to remain in England can be found. The lower stage is groined, and the upper still retains its contemporary wooden balustrade. Much 17th C woodwork is in evidence.

LINGFIELD
Saints Peter & Paul:
187/389438
The church was rebuilt during the 15th C at a time when a college was founded by the lord of the manor. Internally the arrangement leans toward a Kentish style. An interesting lectern holds a chained Bible, secured to prevent theft during the medieval era. Monuments, stalls and a screen.

LOWER KINGSWOOD
The Wisdom of God:
187/248537
A Victorian eccentricity, unique in England, is this replica of a Balkan church with narthex and apse, a great deal of which was brought from Balkan ruins. Totally Byzantine in every respect.

STOKE D'ABERNON
St Mary:
187/129585
Famous for its important series of brasses, that of Sir John D'Abernon (1277) being the earliest surviving in England. Architecturally, the church is pre-Conquest in origin and the S wall dates from this period. There is 12th and 13th C work in evidence, and some remains of 13th C paintings in the chancel. The most notable fixture of later periods is the early 17th C pulpit with tester for producing better accoustics.

Sussex:
East and West

CHICHESTER CATHEDRAL
Holy Trinity:
197/859047
Originally the seat of this diocese was centred at Selsey, founded by Wilfrid in 634, who later became Bishop of York. But William I had it transferred to Chichester, and the new cathedral church was rebuilt here under the direction of Bishop Luffa in 1091. This was unfortunately destroyed by fire 23 years later. Re-erected in 1184, much of the cathedral was again devastated by fire in 1187 and it was not until 1199 that

architectural stability was attained.
Amongst many, the most notable feature of the building is the unique free-standing, 15th C bell-tower with its peal of eight bells, one of which dates from the 16th C. Interestingly, in 1861, part of the 600-year-old tower crashed into the building during a storm. Consequently, that which we see today is a 19th C restoration which took a mere seven years to complete.
Inside, the nave, with Norman arches springing from massive piers, is of the 13th C and flanked either side by chapels, giving the church the appearance of having double aisles. The distinctive pulpitum, erected in 1475, was removed when it was apparent that the spire was about to fall in the 19th C. This has been restored and replaced in modern times. In the S choir aisle are the two most precious possessions of the cathedral: magnificent sculptured tablets depicting Christ at the raising of Lazarus, which probably belonged to the pulpitum of the Norman church.
On the S side of the church are the remains of the early 15th C cloisters, with oak roof. The refectory of the vicars-choral is to the E, while next to the W end of the church is the 14th C gateway to the bishop's palace.

ALFRISTON
St Andrew:
199/522030
A transitional cruciform church built of flint (c1360), it stands away from the village, with a central tower and shingle spire. Inside has been refurnished, but unaltered are the piscina and sedilia of unusual design, and there is an ancient Easter Sepulchre, the focal point of medieval Easter services.

BOSHAM
Holy Trinity:
197/804039
A small but important church which has the distinction of being one of the few featured on the Bayeux Tapestry. Its foundations are historic, originally a Roman site. There was an Irish monastery here before the mission of St Wilfrid. The chancel is part Saxon and part Early English. In 1064, King Harold said prayers here before setting out on his fateful journey to Normandy.

PARHAM
St Peter:
197/059142
Mostly Perpendicular, but remodelled in the 19th C, the church stands in a park next to an Elizabethan house. Nevertheless, good box pews, and a notable 18th C pulpit and screen. Of particular interest is the 14th C font, one of only 35 lead ones in the country; this has Lombardic lettering.

ROTHERFIELD
St Denys:
199/556297
Despite two restorations, the interior of this hilltop church remains totally unspoilt and includes many fine features, including a wall-painting of a Doom on the chancel arch and of an Annunciation over the entrance to the N chapel. The elaborate canopied pulpit of c1630 came from the archbishop of York's private chapel.

SOMPTING
St Mary:
198/162056
Immediately identified by its 11th C Saxon tower with 'Rhenish helm' spire, so named after a group of similar ones found in the Rhine district of Germany. In England, however, it is unique. Architecturally interesting church in other respects, and one should note the transepts, one of which was formed by attaching an otherwise separate Knight Templars chapel.

Tyne and Wear

NEWCASTLE CATHEDRAL
St Nicholas:
88/246640
The bishopric of Newcastle was formed in 1878, following an earlier proposal for the formation of a diocese by no less a person than King Edward VI himself. The church chosen to be the cathedral is among the largest parish churches in England.
Originally erected in 1091, it was destroyed by fire in 1216; consequently the present building is largely 13th C. During the Scottish raids into England it was saved from destruction, unlike many northern churches, by the resourcefulness of the mayor who confined Scottish prisoners in the belfry. In 1784 the church authorities wantonly auctioned off the medieval brasses.
Externally, the most imposing feature is the 15th C lantern tower of unusual and delicate design, the steeple upheld by a crown of flying buttresses. This bears a striking resemblance to that of St Giles, Edinburgh.
Inside, of note is the 14th C crypt, now a chapel, but which was originally an ossuary, or repository of bones, attached to a chantry chapel.

ROKER
St Andrew:
88/406588
A surprising church built in 1906–7, a time little likely to produce a masterpiece of ecclesiastical architecture, but here we have just such a one. A massive and original design by Prior, with Arts and Crafts furnishings to harmonize; Burne-Jones, William Morris, Eric

Gill and Gimson were among those who contributed.

MONKWEARMOUTH
St Peter & St Cuthbert:
88/396577
Typically Saxon in proportion with a tall tower bearing a carved figure on the exterior above the W door which was originally the chancel arch and thus internal! This is all that remains of the first church here, built to serve a Saxon monastery by Benedict Biscop in 674. Inside the church is a fine collection of Saxon carved stone, and recent restoration has unearthed a pane of original stained glass, now identified as the oldest in England, brought over from France by B. Biscop c675.

Warwickshire

COVENTRY CATHEDRAL
St Michael:
140/335791
Of the first church in Coventry nothing is known, except that it served a monastery and according to Canute, was destroyed. The monastery was refounded in the 11th C by Earl Leofric and his wife Godiva, and placed in the charge of Benedictine monks. At the dissolution this church, which at that time sheltered the bishop's cathedra, sharing the privilege with Lichfield, fell into disrepair while a second church built by two brothers and two sisters prospered under the patronage of the trade guilds. Consequently, when the bishopric was revived in 1918, it was this edifice, dedicated to St Michael, which was chosen to be the cathedral.

During World War II the cathedral was largely destroyed by enemy bombs. A new cathedral was commissioned to the design of Sir Basil Spence. The foundation stone for this was laid by Queen Elizabeth II in 1956.

The shell of the medieval church has been preserved, and one entrance to the new building is through this. The tower, however, was undamaged and is 14th C.

Internally, the church is dominated by two main features: the huge tapestry of Christ in Glory by Graham Sutherland and the vast, marvellous John Piper stained glass window of the baptistry, perhaps the cathedral's finest aspect.

HAMPTON LUCY
St Peter ad Vincula:
151/256570
Standing beside Charlcotte Park on the River Avon this is essentially a Victorian church with work by Gilbert Scott and Hutchinson, and also by Rickman who constructed the window tracery in moulded cast-iron and who also built the nearby cast-iron bridge over the Avon. The nave is lofty in

proportion, and has a sensitive plaster vault, giving the impression of a cathedral in miniature.

LOXLEY
St Nicholas:
151/258530
All that an English church should be. Nestling in a valley setting, it was consecrated in 1286 and the chancel is substantially 13th C. The 18th C saw much restoration, leaving a charming interior of box pews, clear glass, and interestingly, a pulpit high-up on a wall which is approached through the vestry.

STRATFORD-UPON-AVON
Holy Trinity:
151/200553
Best appreciated away from the tourist season, it nevertheless retains inside a sense of 'still' beauty. An Early English and Perpendicular town church with a magnificent central tower of excellent proportion. Among many good monuments, Shakespeare's tomb is here.

WARWICK
St Mary:
151/283650
Perhaps the finest of all the county's town churches. The two most notable features are the Gothic-style tower, richly decorated and raised on arches to accommodate the ancient public right of way beneath, and the 15th C Beauchamp chapel with important and richly coloured interior and monuments and its own tiny chantry chapel with pendant vaulting. Also of note are the S nave windows with curiously designed tracery.

West Midlands

BIRMINGHAM CATHEDRAL
St Philip:
139/069870
Built to the design of Thomas Archer in 1711, George II was persuaded to contribute £600 towards the cost of erecting this Neo-Classical style church which became the cathedral on the formation of the diocese in 1905.

Architecturally it lacks force, and is clearly a plain building ornamented with such devices as pilasters with Doric capitals and a balustrade adorned with Grecian urns in order to improve its appearance.

Internally, the nave is separated from the aisles by arcades of coffered arches supported by gilded, fluted piers with Doric capitals and massive plinths, their overall design somewhat marred by the intervening galleries. A prominent cornice is further reinforced with gilding.

Archer's original shallow chancel was replaced by the present one in 1884. Its curved walls and pillars topped with Doric capitals harmonize with the nave

piers. The tower was opened to provide a baptistry during this restoration.

The notable Burne-Jones windows were installed during the last quarter of the 19th C. The artist himself was a native of Birmingham and was baptized in the cathedral.

Wiltshire

SALISBURY CATHEDRAL
Blessed Virgin Mary:
185/144295
Impressive, it is probably the most painted of British cathedrals. It could well be described as poetry in stone, but internally it lacks distinction and is disappointing, perhaps because it is the second cathedral at Salisbury and was undoubtedly built in haste, taking only 48 years to complete!

The first church was erected to the N of the present city at Old Sarum, within the Norman hilltop castle, by Bishop Osmund. It was consecrated in 1092, but almost immediately damaged by lightning. As the exposed site was proving unsatisfactory, it was decided to petition the pope to rebuild it in another place, preferably more sheltered.

The new cathedral was begun in 1220, and the body of Bishop Osmund was moved to the new edifice soon after, where he attracted a stream of pilgrims even though he was not officially canonized until the 15th C.

Architecturally, all the cathedral belongs to the Early English period, and is practically unaltered. Initially, the central tower was squat, barely rising above the roof ridges. Two additional stages were built and the magnificent spire was added in 1334. The spire, 404ft in height, preserves within it the medieval scaffolding. The flying buttresses, to give additional support, are 15th C.

The whole church was dedicated to the Blessed Virgin Mary, although the chapel at the E is also dedicated to the Blessed Trinity. This was the first portion of the building to be completed, being dedicated in 1225. The cloisters were the last phase of the original building to be constructed, in 1270, and are the largest and earliest in the country, though strictly out of place since the cathedral has never been monastic. The Chapter House, much damaged by Cromwell, was added in 1280, and the library over the E wing in 1445.

In the N aisle are the works of what may well be the oldest clock in England.

AVEBURY
St James:
173/099700
Adjoining a famous prehistoric stone circle, the church dates from

Saxon times. Original Saxon remains in nave, aisles 12th C, 13th C work present and the tower is 15th C. Fixtures and fittings include a Norman font and a good 15th C rood loft.

BISHOPS CANNING
St Mary the Virgin:
173/038642
A Norman foundation extensively rebuilt in the 13th C leaving a finely proportioned and interesting church. The present spire, clerestory and upper sacristy are 15th C. Of note is the nave roof of 1670, the early windows at the W end of the N aisle, and the fine arcading for recessed altars in the transept; also the rebuilt Chapel of Our Lady of the Bower with its monuments and Jacobean Holy Table. In the church, too, is a unique 'carrel' or meditation chair.

BRADFORD-ON-AVON
St Laurence:
173/825608
The most well known and probably most visited of the town's two churches. Considered to have been originally erected c700 by St Aldhelm, for many years it stood neglected after having had numerous secular uses from which it still bears the scars. It now stands revealed as one of the oldest and smallest churches in the country. The exterior is decorated with text-book blind arcading while the interior is narrow, mysterious and unadorned except for two carved angel figures high above the chancel arch.

DAUNTSEY
St James:
173/980824
11th C N and S doorways lead into a mainly 14th and 15th C building. The church is important for its contents which include screens of the 14th and 17th C; good painted glass of the 16th C; monuments; and a wood tympanum with a Doom painting which served to point out graphically the manner of after-life expected for those that might feel tempted to succumb to sin in the present.

HORNINGSHAM
Chapel (Congregational):
183/8241
Founded in 1566, it has the distinction of being the oldest surviving chapel in England, and has seen continuous use as a religious building from that date. Although many alterations and some extensions have taken place, notably the removal of the box pews, enough remains of considerable antiquity to be of major interest.

Externally, sunk beside the road under a thatch roof, the chapel resembles a cottage or farm building of the area except for over-size windows. Internally, however, it displays all the hall-marks of any traditional medieval chapel. A wooden gallery of ancient date runs around three sides, of which the panelling to the

114

front is of particularly fine quality; some candle holders remain on the edge of the gallery and gallery pews. The pulpit, the focal point of non-conformist worship, is mounted high on a pedestal and is complete with sounding board. Also original are the hat-pegs which line the rear wall of the men's gallery. Such an arrangement gave rise to the saying 'her eyes stood out like chapel hat-pegs'!

One of the earliest surviving records relating to the Horningsham congregation is a conviction for gathering 'under the pretence of the exercise of religion in other manner, than according to the liturgy and practice of the Church of England'.

STOCKTON
St John the Baptist:
184/983382
The archetypal English church but with an Eastern flavour brought about by the curious arrangement of a solid stone wall, pierced by a central doorway and two squints, closing off the chancel. 15th C in date, a rood loft once existed on the nave side supported on corbels. As to the rest, predominantly 14th C.

Worcestershire (see Herefordshire)

Yorkshire

BRADFORD CATHEDRAL
St Peter:
104/166333
Originally the parish church, it was raised to cathedral status on 25 November 1919.

Historically, a church may have existed on the site as early as the 11th C, but of this, and of the first recorded church of c1200, nothing remains. Much of the medieval fabric dates from the rebuilding during the 14th C.

The massive, square, embattled tower at the W end, with pinnacles, was commenced at the close of the 15th C and completed in 1508, and is the most pleasing aspect of the whole church.

Internally, all is small and dark. The nave is 14th C and the oak roof has been ornamented with heraldic shields and angel corbels, while a few memorials grace the walls. This contrasts with the modern work which took place in the Horningsham 1960s and saw a complete redevelopment of the cathedral E end. The scheme, imaginative in concept, using local stone, involved the demolition of the old chancel and the opening up of the Leventhorpe and Bolling chapels to form a part of a continuous

ambulatory. It provided a new chancel beneath a lantern tower of short stature, the Lady Chapel, the chapel of the Holy Spirit, St Aidan's chapel and the Chapter House, together with two new entrances.

RIPON CATHEDRAL
St Peter & St Wilfrid:
99/314712
A Saxon monastery was founded here in the 7th C, and shortly afterwards St Wilfrid built a stone church of which the crypt survives. This was burned by the Danes in the 9th C and rebuilt by 934, when it was known as one of the sanctuary churches. The Normans did much damage during their 'harrying of the north' and it remained ruined until 1080. During the 14th C Scottish raiders caused a great deal of vandalism, and Cromwell's men 300 years later smashed all the ancient glass. In 1604 James I re-established the Chapter and placed the church in the care of deans and canons. It was adopted as the cathedral of a new diocese in 1836.

Architecturally, the W front dates from 1220. Originally all three towers were capped by wooden spires, but part of the central tower collapsed in 1450 and following rebuilding the spire was not replaced. In 1664 the western spires were removed for fear of similar collapse.

Internally, there are two features of particular note. The magnificent pulpitum which divides the nave from the choir was built in 1500. The coloured statuary has been restored in the present century, and brings back to the church some of the brilliance of medieval times. The other feature of note is the crossing, remarkable for possessing two arches of the earlier church of the 12th C and two of the 15th C.

SHEFFIELD CATHEDRAL
St Peter & St Paul:
111/354873
The cathedral occupies the site of a church founded in the reign of Henry I, but during the 18th C the fabric was so neglected that it became a total ruin. In 1805 the building was wholly reconstructed. The present century has seen much enlargement of the building into a light and spacious cathedral of great attraction.

The oaken sedilia of late 15th C date is the sole link with the original church. The nave (with aisles), the clerestory (without triforium), and the transepts were erected in the 19th C.

On the N side a lantern has been built. Steps lead to a handsome regimental chapel. A crypt chapel beneath, actually on a level with the street, is dedicated to the Holy Spirit.

The modern gilded cathedra has a figure of Christ. The vaulting is embellished with gilded angels and bosses. Altars stand N and S, and there is a Tudor memorial to an earl of Shrewsbury.

WAKEFIELD CATHEDRAL
All Saints:
104/334207
A Saxon church existed on this site, of which a Saxon cross dated 960, now in a York museum, may be the sole relic. This church was mentioned in the Domesday Book and was replaced by another church in the 12th C. Two hundred years later part of the building was demolished by the fall of the central tower; the new church was consecrated in 1329. In the following century the nave was lengthened and a tower added. In the 15th C a clerestory was added to the nave and the choir again rebuilt and the nave aisles extended. The church was further enlarged eastwards at the beginning of the present century following the adoption of the cathedral on the formation of a new diocese in 1887.

Architecturally, the exterior is dominated by the tall, graceful crocketted spire which was erected in the 15th C.

Recently, the church has seen the addition of a detached hall extension at the E end, erected as a memorial to Bishop Eric Tracey.

Internally, little remains of any of the previous churches, two pillars in the N side of the nave being the sole survivors of the earliest churches. The chancel arch and nave arcading is 15th C, with the upper portion dating from 1635. There is also a handsome modern rood. Font cover and pulpit are early 18th C. The S transept displays a replica of the Saxon cross of 960.

YORK MINSTER
St Peter:
105/604524
The largest of English cathedrals, it grew from a small wooden church erected in the year 627 for the baptism of Edwin, king of Northumbria by Paulinus, chaplain to Ethelburga, daughter of the converted Christian king of Kent, Ethelbert and Edwin's bride.

This wooden structure was probably replaced by one of stone at an early date, and it is supposed that this was destroyed during William I's harrowing of the north. At the end of the 11th C it was rebuilt by the then Norman archbishop, but within 40 years was so damaged by fire as to become ruinous. Towards the end of the 12th C it was again rebuilt. The present church for the most part owes its origin to the masons of the 13th, 14th and 15th C.

In modern times, more than any other cathedral, York has suffered a number of vicissitudes, in particular a series of major fires in 1829, 1840 and more recently in 1984. A major restoration programme had to be instigated in the mid-1970s when serious damage to the fabric was discovered.

Internally, some of the more notable features are the ceilings and roof bosses. The nave is of 14th C date and wooden, the N

transept ceiling has 15th C bosses, but is otherwise a modern restoration. In the Chapter House, however, adjoining the N transept, the immense wooden roof, 58ft in width, unsupported by any central column, ranks among the great engineering achievements of medieval times and was built between 1286 and 1340.

The Minster retains a greater quantity of ancient stained glass than any other cathedral. The W window dates from 1338; in the N transept is the famous 'five sisters' window; the E window contains much 15th C work, and on the N side of the nave, a 12th C panel may be the second oldest surviving stained glass in the country.

There are relics of the earlier churches in the crypt, and an interpretation centre has been constructed in the undercroft which displays the Roman city of Ebor on which the church was built, as well as a fine collection of Yorkshire church plate.

Outside, the great central tower was raised in 1480, the SW in 1456 and the balancing NW tower was completed in 1474. The magnificent W front of beautiful proportion was erected between 1317 and 1340, although the actual W doors are a 19th C addition.

In the 20th C it has been said that York Minster is in danger of losing its Christian identity, under the overwhelming number of visitors which flock to what has now become a showpiece of tourism.

ALMONDBURY
All Hallows:
110/168151
Essentially a late 15th C church with some 13th C work. The very fine nave ceiling has decorative bosses and a carved gilded prayer inscription dated 1522 running round it like a frieze. A tall ornate font cover, required by medieval Church law to protect the 'holy water' from theft, is one of the best in the county.

BEDALE
St Gregory:
99/265885
A truly outstanding building with wall-paintings, vaulted crypt and an early 14th C tower built for parochial defense against Border raiders, complete with evidence of a portcullis to protect the internal staircase.

BRAMHOPE
Ded Un (Chapel):
104/248436
With a simple, graceful interior, this chapel stands in grounds which once belonged to the hall, now demolished. It was one of the first Puritan chapels in the country, built in 1645 by the lord of the manor, an early supporter of the 'Commonwealth' cause.

COWTHORPE
St Michael:
105/427528
Attractive late 15th C church. Inside is a rare treasure, a similarly dated portable oak Easter Sepulchre which would be processed around the parish and then placed in the church, where a vigil would be kept by it from Good Friday until Easter Sunday. It would then be decorated and the curtain opened to reveal the tomb empty, signifying 'Christ is Risen'.

COXWOLD
St Michael:
100/534772
Noted for its distinctive octagonal W tower. Contains magnificent memorials to the local gentry, and a unique 17th C looped T-shaped communion rail built to fit into the existing chancel space left after the erection of some of the major monuments.

EASBY
St Agatha:
92/185004
This long, low building with bell-cote stands near the gatehouse of a ruined priory of slightly later date. Enlarged in the 15th C when the S aisle and large vaulted porch (with a priests' living chamber overhead) were added.

HEALAUGH
St John:
105/498479
Mainly Norman with a sumptuous S doorway showing 'Christ in Majesty' and the 'Orders of Heaven and Earth', including entwining beasts of hell on the capitals. Very fine set of corbels which supposedly represent evil spirits outside the church.

HEPTONSTALL
Octagonal Chapel (Methodist):
103/987282
The epitome of northern Methodist architecture. Rugged, solid, perched on a hillside with spectacular views, this is one of the country's oldest continually-used chapels. Built in 1764 to the favoured octagonal plan, John Wesley made many visits here to preach to huge congregations.

HUBBERHOLME
St Michael:
98/925783
An old church with 16th C rood loft, one of only two in Yorkshire. Here the priest would conduct parts of certain services under the great 'rood' or crucifix hung above.

KIRKBURTON
All Hallows:
110/197125
Much 13th C work with 15th–17th C woodwork. A squint for viewing the altar is believed to have opened out from an anchorite's cell.

KIRKDALE
St Gregory:
100/676858
A church with Saxon origins and the most superb Saxon sundial in England. The lengthy inscription reads 'Orm Gamal's Son bought St Gregory's Minster when it was all broken and fallen and let it be made anew from the ground to Christ and St Gregory in Edward's days, the king and Tosti's days, the Earl.' Inside, stone benches run around the walls, reflecting the days when the body of the church had no pews and people stood for services, leading to the expression 'the weakest go to the wall'.

KNARESBOROUGH
Chapel of Our Lady of the Crag:
104/3457
Unique single-cell shrine dug out of the wayside cliff by licence dated 1409. A later, over-life-size figure of a knight drawing his sword guards the entrance.

LASTINGHAM
St Mary:
94/728905
Stands on the site of a monastery established by St Cedd in 654, refounded in 1078 by Abbot Stephen of Whitby before moving the community to York to set up St Mary's Abbey. Fine Norman chancel with apse. The most remarkable feature of this church is a complete unspoilt 11th C crypt built over the grave of St Cedd as a shrine for pilgrims – and being unique itself as a complete church with apsidal chancel and nave with side aisles.

PICKERING
St Peter & St Paul:
100/799840
A large 13th–15th C building with Norman origins. Its outstanding feature is the vast array of mid-15th C wall-paintings covering all the upper nave walls. These were important visual aids in medieval churches and illustrated for the illiterate people biblical scenes and the lives of the saints.

ROTHERHAM
Bridge Chapel of Our Lady:
111/427927
Standing on a medieval bridge, it is one of only five such chapels left in England. Built in 1485, it was used by travelling pilgrims.

SPROTBOROUGH
St Mary:
111/539020
An Early English building with a fine 13th C piscina for pouring away unused communion wine, sedilia, or clergy seats, and credence shelf where the bread and wine was placed before being taken to the altar for consecration.

TONG
St James:
104/219305
A complete Classical-style church built in 1727 by the lord of the manor, although archaeological evidence shows Norman foundations. Very good Georgian furnishings including three-decker pulpit and sounding board and squire's pew with fireplace to keep the family warm through the immense 18th C sermons.

WENSLEY
Holy Trinity:
99/093896
A church with a remarkably diverse selection of fixtures and fittings, but its crowning glory must be the large free-standing 15th C wooden reliquary taken from Easby Abbey. Containing some part of a saint, it would be taken around the parish for people to make offerings in exchange for a blessing.

YORK
St Martin-cum-Gregory, Micklegate:
105/598516
Stretching back into antiquity, with re-used Roman masonry and a Roman tombstone incorporated in its structure of many periods. Its 18th C fittings include a large pew box and cupboard for keeping the bread 'dole' before distribution to the unfortunate of the parish after the service.

WALES

Clwyd

ST ASAPH'S CATHEDRAL
St Asaph:
116/039744
About 560 St Kentigern founded a monastery in this district where St Asaph succeeded him as bishop. The church, rebuilt by the Normans, was destroyed in the 13th C by the English and in the following century by Glyndwr. The building suffered during the time of Cromwell, and in 1714 as the result of a storm which stripped the roof. In 1779 the Chapter House was demolished and the building left in a ruinous condition. Restoration was undertaken by Gilbert Scott at the end of the 19th C.

A memorial in the churchyard commemorates those who translated the Bible and Prayer Book into Welsh in the 16th C, and the library includes among its possessions a New Testament of 1567 in Welsh, and other rare books.

BODELWYDDAN
St Margaret:
116/004754
Often erroneously referred to as 'the marble church', it is in fact constructed of local white limestone, although the interior of this fantastical church, with its 202ft W spire, contains much marble. Built by John Gibson between 1856 and 1860, it is lavish, ornate and the interior is expensive and richly carved.

MOLD
St Mary:
117/236643
One of the most notable medieval churches in the county. 16th and 18th C work predominates; fine timber roof; good glass of early periods; and of the modern work, an unusual art deco War Memorial Chapel.

RUABON
New Bridge Chapel
(Baptist):
117/3043
A hansome building of traditional chapel design, inscribed and dated 1826 on the exterior in English and Welsh. Inside, the baptistry is actually sited within the large pulpit. Many pew-backs retain small metal rings for individual communion glasses.

WORTHENBURY
St Deiniol:
117/419463
A splendid, mellow, red-brick 18th C church with fine W tower and an apsidal chancel. Internally unrestored with box pews, two of which in the chancel retain fireplaces.

Dyfed

ST DAVID'S CATHEDRAL
St David:
158/752254
Dewi Sant, St David, founded a monastery here in the 6th C. The Normans gave the church into the charge of canons, consecrating their first cathedral building in 1131. The fabric was unfortunately restored in the 18th C by John Nash, and corrected by Sir Gilbert Scott in the 19th C.

The tower collapsed in 1220 and only its lowest stage remains; the second is 14th C and the uppermost is 16th C.

Inside, the 12th C nave is unusual in having round arches. For the most, the rest is of 14th, 15th and 16th C date, and some of the more notable features include the cathedra, with chaplains' seats, and wooden sedilia of beautiful Perpendicular design erected in the early 16th C.

West of the Lady Chapel the ambulatory once formed the eastern boundary of a rectangular space open to the sky. In the 16th C this was made into the Trinity chapel, with fine fan-vaulting. Here the relics of St David now rest in a casket. They were discovered, secreted in the fabric, in the 19th C. The recess which they now occupy originally provided the pilgrims' view of the shrine standing in the presbytery.

CAREW CHERITON
St Mary:
157/046027
Large cruciform plan church, predominantly 14th C with Perpendicular and Decorated period windows, it stands with medieval charnel house and rectory. Inside are interesting fittings; tombs; sanctuary tiles of c1500.

LLANDOVERY (Llanfair-y-Bryn)
St Mary:
160/770352
Erected on the site of a Roman fort, this church has unusual proportions which make it appear like a great tithe barn to which a 13th C tower has been attached. External gargoyles and parapet added c1500.

TENBY
St Mary:
158/132005
Probably the most complete Perpendicular church in the county, although it was originally a 13th C church and still retains tower and octagonal spire of this period. W door has nice ogee arch and is the same date as the S porch c1500.

Glamorgan: South, Mid and West

LLANDAFF CATHEDRAL
St Peter & St Paul:
171/156781
Teilo, a missionary bishop of the 6th C, founded a monastery here, with school. He was related to St David and was accompanied by his cousin Dubricius or Dyfrig, who shares with him credit for founding the first church here. Dyfrig later retired to Bardsey Island where he lived as a hermit. After his death his bones were brought back to the cathedral in 1120.

The building suffered considerable damage from a land mine in World War II, far exceeding that inflicted upon it in previous centuries by Reformers, Cromwellians, and the tasteless restoration work of the 17th C.

The W front is 13th C and has figures of Christ the King and St Teilo. The pinnacles of the 15th C N tower were blown down in a storm in 1703, doing much damage, and the S tower fell before a second storm twenty years later, to be restored in the 19th C. Along the S wall of the nave and continuing on the N wall are the sculptured heads of British sovereigns.

The detached Norman belfry, ruinous since the 15th C, may be seen near the Deanery, and the ruined gateway which once gave access to the episcopal palace now serves as entrance to the school.

Internally, the church is dominated by Epstein's impressive Majesta set against the concrete organ case supported by light concrete arches designed by George Pace, marking the division between nave and choir. Pre-Raphaelite figures from the choir stalls decorate the organ case.

The St Illtyd chapel beneath the NW tower has a Rossetti triptych above its altar, and at the E extremity of the N aisle in the St Dyfrig chapel are six beautiful della robbia panels designed by Burne-Jones.

CRYNANT
Gelli Dochllithe Chapel
(Baptist):
159/539505
Erected in rusticated stone, a plaque records: 'Codre Rhos built 1764, Independent Chapel, Rebuilt in the year 1855 by H. Williams, Contractors'. Inside, much colour, box pews yellow with red top rails.

EWENNY
St Michael:
170/913778
Originally part of a Benedictine monastery founded c1141, although the church is c1120. Nave forms parish church and is still mostly 12th C, as is crossing, transepts and W wall which shortened the nave. Aisle and porch 16th C. Internally, there is 14th C wood screen, 16th C linen-fold panelling, 12th C font.

LLANTWIT MAJOR
St Illtyd:
170/966687
An amazingly long church of four distinct sections: the collegiate church in the chancel and nave (with aisle and W tower); the parochial church; a W portion; and an extreme W galilee, now in ruins. Of many dates, it contains a fine, carved Jesse Tree; 13th–15th C wall-paintings, and a splendid collection of Celtic crosses and medieval tombs.

OXWICH
St Illtyd:
159/504861
An isolated cliff-top church of diminutive proportion whose chief glory is the painted chancel ceiling executed at the expense of Dame Lilian Baylis of Old Vic fame.

Gwent

NEWPORT CATHEDRAL
St Woolos:
171/308876
The church served the local parish until it was made the pro-cathedral of the diocese of Monmouth in 1929. It was later raised to cathedral status in 1949.

A church was first erected here in the late 6th C by Gwynllyw as an act of penitence; St Woolos is a corruption of that name. A Norman church replacing any earlier buildings was burnt down in 1462.

The Norman builders apparently preserved the Saxon church, building on to its E wall and effectively providing a chapel between tower and nave. The present fabric inside, however, dates from the 13th C and only an octagonal window in the S wall survives from any early building.

The magnificent arch leading to the nave is Norman as are the arcades of the nave with their chamfered capitals and splayed windows. The aisles are 15th C.

The chancel was restored in the 19th C and extended in the present century. The rose window above the altar has glass by John Piper.

LLANFACHES
St Dyfrig:
172/434917
Although of medieval origin, it was completely restored in the Arts & Crafts style of 1908 by Groves, retaining only coloured glass and a carved screen.

SKENFRITH
St Bridget:
161/456203
Attached to a lofty square tower capped with a splendid timber two-stage pyramid belfry, more at home in the county of Herts. Inside, the church's most remarkable treasure is a magnificent 15th C cope.

Gwynedd

BANGOR CATHEDRAL
St Deiniol:
115/581721
The first church was erected in 525 by St Deiniol to serve a small community of missionary monks. In 545 St Deiniol was made a bishop and the church subsequently became a cathedral. Consequently, Bangor cathedral, on the site of Deiniol's church, possibly occupies the most ancient cathedral site in the entire British Isles.

St Deiniol's church was destroyed by the Normans in 1071 to be replaced by a grander, but yet small, aisless church which in turn was destroyed in the 13th C as was its successor in the 15th C.

The tower is 16th C, and of any Norman churches, only a blocked window in the S wall of the chancel and a buttress survive.

The cathedral shelters the plain, 12th C tomb of Prince Owain Gwynedd, and a medieval carved figure of our Lord known as the Mostyn Christ. Other treasures include a charter of Elizabeth I and a finely preserved Pontifical of Bishop Anian, who baptized Edward II.

ABERFRAW (Llangwyfan)
St Gwyfan:
114/336683
A small single-cell church of 12th C date, sited on a tiny island, easily reached at low tide. Interestingly, the N wall contains 16th C arcading which suggests a later aisle was added and presumably since demolished.

CLYNNOG FAWR
St Beuno:
115/416497
An imposing Perpendicular edifice whose rich interior is derived from its importance as a shrine on the pilgrim's route to Bardsey Island.

The passage leading to St Beuno's chapel survives from the original 7th C church.

LLANBEDR
Salem Chapel (Baptist):
124/5826
In keeping with the original strictures and needs of Baptist chapels, this beautiful and ancient building is set, as so many Welsh Baptist places of worship, near to a stream for the purpose of baptism by total immersion. A simple, calm interior dominated by the pulpit.

LLANDUDNO
St Tudno:
115/792821
A long, low, simple church almost chapel-like, with bell-cote, sited on a cliff-top. The most notable feature is the huge canopied preaching pulpit on the S side, a relic of the days when vast congregations gathered to attend to the word.

LLANGADWALADR
St Cadwaladr:
114/383693
An important historical church of 7th C date under ancient royal patronage of Cadfar (d. c625) and the royal chieftain Cadwaladr, his grandson. Nave dates from 12th C; chancel 14th C; 15th C window; 17th C chapel.

Powys

BRECON CATHEDRAL
St John the Evangelist:
160/045290
Originally a church served by Benedictine monks, it was raised to cathedral status in 1923.

The tower is 13th C. Internally, the severely designed nave is 14th C and while the rood screen is gone, the door to it and the supporters survive. The choir contains fine 13th C work, with five lancets above the high altar. On the N side is the chapel of St Keyne, and this is perhaps the most interesting part of the church, with barrel roof and 14th C effigy. It was first dedicated to the two patron saints of shoemakers, St Crispin and St Crispinian. The N transept now shelters a military chapel and contains triple lancets and a squint to afford a view of the high altar. The S transept has two bays and the restored chapel of St Lawrence.

CHAPEL-Y-FFIN
Ded Un:
161/253314
Curious tiny late 18th C church described by Kilvert as 'the old chapel, short, stout and boxy, with its little bell turret (the whole building reminding one of an owl), the quiet peaceful chapel yard sheltered by seven great solemn yews'.

LLANELIEU
St Ellyw:
161/185342
Predominantly 13th C, this church retains inside a sturdy rood screen, loft and 14th C tympanum on which painting survives. From an earlier church are two pillar stones of 7th and 9th C date.

OLD RADNOR
St Stephen:
148/250591
Perpendicular church restored sensitively during the Victorian era. Imposing tower and beacon turret. Inside, features of note include medieval choir stalls; carved screen; the oldest organ case in Britain (c1500); interesting Easter sepulchre in N chapel; hatchments; 18th C painting of Aaron and Moses; and a font fashioned from a huge block of igneous rock, which is probably of pre-Christian religious significance.

SCOTLAND

Borders

ABBEY ST BATHANS
St Baothan:
67/758624
Erected on the site of a 12th C Cistercian nunnery, parts of which are incorporated into the present parish church. Also retains an early tomb of a prioress.

COLDINGHAM
67/903659
Originally a priory founded in 1098, which was later put in charge of Benedictine monks in the 12th C. Twice attacked, plundered and fired by the English; Cromwell later did much damage. Mainly 16th C with earlier work, restored 19th C. This is one of the oldest churches in Scotland still in use.

ECCLES
St Mary:
74/764413
Near to the site of an important Cistercian convent founded in 1155, this large parish church, built in 1774, displays a handsome spire unusual for the period. A bell is dated 1659.

Central

ABERFOYLE
57/524011
The ruin of the old church is of particular note, and the churchyard which features in Scott's *Rob Roy* contains cast-iron mort safes, designed to foil the activities of body-snatchers seeking specimens to sell to the medical profession for research.

Dumfries and Galloway

MONREITH
St Medana:
83/365400
Two chapels of the same dedication stand opposite each other over a promontory and commemorate the maritime feat of the patron maiden who reputedly floated between them on a rock. The chapel here is unique in being hewn out of the stone cliff and excavations have yielded pilgrims'

badges and a sandstone statue which is possibly a representation of St Medana.

RUTHWELL
85/101683
A pleasant church of classical design, it is particularly noted for the 'Ruthwell Cross', one of the foremost monuments of Dark Age Europe. Standing 18ft high, it was discovered under the church floor, placed there in the 17th C. Of 7th C date, there is inscribed upon it a runic text, a portion of the oldest poem in English literature, and numerous figure scenes. Now displayed in a specially designed apsidal annexe attached to the church.

WIGTOWN
St Machutus:
83/435556
Of ancient origin, it was rebuilt in 1730, but became ruinous and a new church was erected alongside it in 1853. 10th C cross-shafts; remarkable memorial to 'Wigtown Martyrs', two women who were tied to a stake and drowned by the rising tide for their adherence to the covenanting faith.

Fife

DUNFERMLINE ABBEY
65/090874
A handsome and noble church in which are buried nine kings, five queens, six princes and two princesses. Extensively rebuilt and restored following successive sackings, it incorporates the earlier 11th C building and the nave is pure Romanesque. 13th C work and later periods. The central tower restored in the early 19th C. The extensive and important monastic buildings lay to the S of the abbey.

LEUCHARS
St Andrew:
59/454215
The 11th C apse and chancel display the finest example of Norman work in Scotland. In the charge of a monastic order from 1171–99. 13th C tower and belfry. Restored 1914. Inside, crusaders' tombs and finely carved grotesques.

Grampian

ABERDEEN CATHEDRAL
St Andew:
38/937061
Historically, the cathedral is notable in being the descendant of a chapel founded in Bishop Skinner's house, in which Bishop Seabury was consecrated the first bishop of the American Episcopal Church in 1784. Bishop Skinner's private chapel then served the small congregation of penalized Episcopalians in Aberdeen until the erection of a separate chapel on adjacent ground in 1792 and, in the following century, the present church.
Architecturally, the nave is 19th C and the chancel and sanctuary are a 20th C rebuild. The foundation stone, laid by Joseph Kennedy when American Ambassador to Britain, is N of the high altar, and the American association is further reinforced in the roof of the N aisle which is decorated with the arms of the 48 American States.
The S aisle ends in the Suther Chapel of the Reserved Sacrament and is entered through a finely decorated screen. The roof is embellished with the heraldic arms of the 48 families of NE Scotland who remained loyal to the church throughout its persecution.

ARBUTHNOTT
St Ternan:
45/802747
A magnificent cruciform church consecrated in 1242. Of this building, what survives can be seen in the chancel. Rebuilt and restored. Notable for the aisle which forms the lower stage to a tower erected by Sir Robert Arbuthnott c1471 to house a portable altar which he had obtained under licence from Pope Innocent VIII. Priest chamber above.

CHAPEL OF GARIOCH
St Mary:
38/732236
Originally a private chantry chapel of early date. It was confirmed as a regular chapel by the Abbot of Lindores in 1195, and became a parish church in 1583.

CRATHIE
44/265949
The second church here, opened in June 1895, it replaces a plain 19th C 'kirk'. Situated near to Balmoral, this is a 'royal' church insomuch as it is used by the royal family when in residence. Queen Victoria favoured it, and it contains many memorials to the royal family. John Brown was buried here in the churchyard near to the ruins of the medieval church.

Highland

INVERNESS CATHEDRAL
St Andrew:
26/664448
Erected in 1866 to the design of Dr Alexander Ross, this was the first cathedral built in Britain after the Reformation. The W end is flanked by two massive towers of rose-coloured stone. Consisting of nave, transepts and apsidal chancel, the nave arches are supported by pillars of polished granite. A finely-carved oaken screen separates nave from chancel. The baptistry beneath the S tower contains a life-size angel font copied from Thorvaldsen's font in Copenhagen. There is a 15th C panel by Sano di Pietro depicting the Virgin and Child with Franciscan saints, and five icons presented by a czar of Russia.

CANISBAY
12/344729
Considerably restored and rebuilt, this church dates from the 15th C, of which the fortified tower survives. Externally plain, it contains inside a monument (1560) to the Groat family, which was found under the floor of the church in the 19th C.

EDDERTON
21/710846
A Premonstratensian abbey was founded here in 1221 but was later removed to another site. The church now dates from 1742 and was restored in 1794. Fine stone spire.

REAY
St Mary:
11/966648
18th C church built in the typical 'Caithness style' with external tower-stairs and fine contemporary loft and pulpit. Nearby are the ruins of a 12th C chapel.

Lothian

EDINBURGH CATHEDRAL
St Mary:
66/257734
The diocese was founded by Charles I with St Giles as its cathedral, but this arrangement lasted only a short time. After the repeal of the Penal Laws, St Paul's church became the pro-cathedral in 1874 until the present cathedral was consecrated in 1879. It was designed by Sir George Gilbert Scott in the Gothic style. The central spire and those at each side of the W front were completed in the 20th C. The rood was designed by Sir Robert Lorimer. The N transept is the baptistry, the S a War Memorial chapel; a further chapel is dedicated to King Charles and All Souls. The clerestory

window displays the armorial bearings of noble Scottish families.

EDINBURGH
St Giles:
66/255736
Formerly the cathedral church of Edinburgh. Of Norman origin, this was destroyed in 1385 and subsequently rebuilt. Predominantly 15th C. Features of note include the tower with flying buttresses supporting a crown and miniature steeple, and a number of interesting memorials.

DALKEITH
St Nicholas:
66/329674
12th C origins, it was raised to the status of collegiate church during the 15th C and rebuilt. Inside: medieval fittings, a restored apse, and the unique Morton monument with an effigy of the 1st Earl of Morton in parliamentary dress and not armour, the only effigy so clothed in Britain.

HADDINGTON
St Mary:
66/518736
Originally Saxon, rebuilt 1134 of red sandstone, it was again rebuilt 14th C to a cruciform plan. Rich in architectural details. Suffered extensively in the 16th C and was only restored to glory in the 1970s. Inside are many features, and the church is associated with a number of notable Scots, including Thomas Carlyle.

Strathclyde

GLASGOW CATHEDRAL
St Mary the Virgin:
64/602657
Dedicated to St Mary, with a side chapel to St Anne, the cathedral perpetuates the dedication of another church which was second in importance to St Mungo's cathedral in the latter part of the 16th and 17th C.

Designed by Gilbert Scott, the church was built between 1870 and 1884. It contains the only peal of bells in the city. In Early English style with Early Decorated overtones, the attractive spire to the design of John Oldred Scott was completed in 1893.

The interior is simple, with open timber roof beams, which form a wooden groin vault at the crossing.

As well as the chapel of St Anne to the N of the high altar, there are two further chapels in each transept.

OBAN CATHEDRAL
St John:
49/854307
Architecturally an ill-designed building, it consists of two separate parts joined without harmony. The nave of grey stone is the first parish church, consecrated in

1864. The sanctuary, choir, chapel, sacristy and aisle, of red stone, are portions of an uncompleted scheme commenced in 1908 to the design of James Chalmers. A tower above the entrance at the SE was intended but never realized, and the central tower was never completed as the foundations proved unable to bear the weight.

The united buildings were opened for worship in 1910 and given cathedral status in 1928, while the crossing was finished with a lantern and opened in 1958. Considerable renovation and improvement was carried out in 1968.

BOTHWELL
St Bride:
64/704586
Until 1933 when they were joined, two churches existed adjacent, the old dating from 1398, the second 1833. A plaque in the church commemorates Sir Henry Hozier, whose daughter Clementine married Winston Churchill.

DOUGLAS
St Bride:
71/835310
Founded in the 12th C and rebuilt 1390, it is now a picturesque ruin in the care of the DoE. It is notable for its many monuments and an unusual clock tower with clock dated 1565, a gift of Mary Queen of Scots.

Tayside

DUNDEE CATHEDRAL
St Paul:
54/3039
The cathedral, built in the Gothic style, was designed by Gilbert Scott and consecrated in 1855, becoming in 1904 the cathedral of a diocese previously served by the cathedral at Brechin.

The nave has arcades of slender columns bearing pointed arches. The apsidal chancel contains a reredos of Italian mosaics above its high altar. A brass in the centre of the choir marks the grave of the founder-bishop. The N transept has an altar and reredos from a former mission church and the Lady Chapel reredos depicts the Annunciation. The font stands on a pedestal which once belonged to Lindores Abbey, and a cabinet has carved panels from the same abbey's choir stalls.

PERTH CATHEDRAL
St Ninian:
53/115239
The cathedral, to the design of Butterfield, was partially completed and opened for worship in 1850, serving the united diocese of St Andrews, Dunkeld and Dunblane. The building was not completed until the 20th century.

The lofty nave and chancel are in the Gothic style separated by a

stone screen bearing a rood, designed by Sir Ninian Comper. The clerestory windows contain heraldic glass depicting the arms of the benefactors. The reredos of the high altar and double sedilia are made of Aberfeldy stone, the baldacchino of Cornish granite. In the sanctuary is the tomb and bronze effigy of Bishop Torrey, who was Primus at the beginning of the present century and responsible for the enlargement of the cathedral.

BRECHIN
St David:
54/603598
Formerly a cathedral of early date on the site of Culdee Abbey. Predominantly 13th C with 12th C work in evidence. Partly ruinous, the choir serves as the parish church. Notable cross-head c900, and of particular interest one of only two round towers in Scotland (10th–11th C).

GUTHRIE
St Mary:
54/567505
Once the possession of Abroath Abbey, it was purchased in 1479 by Sir David Guthrie who raised it to a collegiate church. Internally, many medieval fittings.

KETTINS
St Mary:
53/238391
A church was consecrated here in 1249 which was subordinate to Culper Abbey. Two unusual features: detached belfry with 16th C bell, and a lych-gate. A large 9ft sculptured stone is preserved in the churchyard.

Western Isles

KIRKWALL CATHEDRAL
(Orkney Isles, Mainland)
St Magnus:
6/449109
The first church erected here was founded in 1137 by Rognvald Jarl III as a penance for his uncle, who murdered St Magnus in 1115. In 1926 the remains of both the saint and the founder were found hidden in the fabric.

Cruciform in plan, the tower was built in 1525 on Early English arches. The spire was destroyed by lightning in 1671.

The nave, narrow in proportion to its height, was probably built by the same masons who raised Durham cathedral, and possibly Dunfermline Abbey. The round arches are supported by massive stone pillars with undecorated capitals. The 13th C choir ends in an E wall pierced by four lancets and a rose window inserted in 1511. Clerestory and vault are also 13th C. The S aisle has a 16th C crocketted tomb. There are some remains of the episcopal palace where King Haakon of Norway

died in 1263 after ceding the Hebrides to Scotland.

EUROPIE (Lewis)
St Moluag:
48/519654
Of ancient origin this church is now mainly 12th C. The church is in the care of the Scottish Episcopal Church who restored and re-roofed it in this century. David Livingstone presented his prayer book to this church, which can be seen today in St Peter's Episcopal church, Stornoway.

IONA
St Mary:
48/286244
In 563 St Columba arrived on the island of Iona from Ireland and established a monastic missionary centre, and it is from this that the present church was derived.

Formerly a cathedral, it has seen much restoration. Originally built in the 13th C, of this building the tower can be seen resting on the Norman arches, but its windows are of later date. Five rounded-headed windows can be seen above the pointed doorway of the W end and the sacristy has an elaborately carved doorway of 1500. The Chapter House with Scriptorium above has a 13th C doorway, and the capitals of the nave arcades are particularly notable. In the chancel are the tombs of two abbots of the early 16th C, and a 14th C sedilia. A polished stone kept behind a grill is reputedly the pillow of St Columba.

RODELL (Harris)
St Clement:
18/047832
Fine cruciform structure of ambitious design. Mainly early 16th C it incorporates work of an earlier church, and is probably attributable to Alexander MacLeod of Dunvegan, whose tomb is in S side choir. Now in the care of the DoE.